MANAGING COLLEGES AND UNIVERSITIES BY OBJECTIVES

*A Concise Guide to Understanding and
Implementing MBO in Higher Education*

L. James Harvey, Ph.D.
Director of the Education Division
McManis Associates, Inc.
Washington, D.C.

Published by:

Ireland Educational Corporation
2275 East Arapahoe Road
Suite 313
Littleton, Colorado

L. James Harvey, Ph.D.
McManis Associates, Inc.
1201 Connecticut Avenue, N.W.
Washington, D.C. 20036
Telephone: (202) 296-1355

Library of Congress Catalogue Card Number: LC 76-6655
International Standard Book Number: 0-89103-015-8

First Edition

PREFACE

Since 1973, McManis Associates, Inc. has been offering national workshops on Management by Objectives (MBO). In addition, the firm has assisted institutions of higher education to implement this and other management systems for years. Dr. L. James Harvey, Director of the Education Division, has spearheaded this effort.

In 1974, Dr. Harvey wrote *Management by Objectives in Higher Education: A Guide to Implementation.* This publication has been exceptionally well received and has undergone several reprintings. Because of the rapid development of new management systems in higher education and advanced technology in MBO, Dr. Harvey felt the need to develop a new book with more up-to-date material.

This book updates the reader on the latest developments and ideas on MBO in higher education. The objectives of the book are to assist the reader in:

- *Developing a current knowledge of MBO;*

- *Understanding how to implement MBO;*

- *Developing a skill in writing objectives; and*

- *Understanding the linkage of MBO, MIS, PPBS, IBO, and evaluation.*

This book is purposely written in a clear, concise fashion and is condensed so that the busy president, faculty member, trustee, administrator, or other interested reader can gain a clear understanding of this most significant management concept in a short period of time.

Gerald L. McManis
President
McManis Associates, Inc.

i

ABOUT THE AUTHOR

Dr. L. James Harvey is an honors graduate of Hope College in Holland, Michigan. He received his M.A. and Ph.D. degrees from Michigan State University and has served in top administrative positions in both two- and four-year institutions. He has been Dean of Students at Hope College and Dean of Arts and Sciences at the Inter-American University of Puerto Rico. Dr. Harvey has also been Vice President of Student Affairs at William Rainey Harper College in Palatine, Illinois, and President of Prince George's Community College in Maryland.

At Harper College and Prince George's Community College, Dr. Harvey had several years of practical experience in implementing the MBO concept. He is a widely known speaker on the subject and has lectured on MBO at colleges and universities from coast to coast. In addition, he has delivered numerous speeches and papers on MBO at national conferences and conventions.

Dr. Harvey has assisted many colleges, universities, and governmental agencies in implementing the MBO concept. He has directed the McManis Associates, Inc. national MBO workshop program which has had hundreds of participants from over 40 states and several foreign countries. His practical experience in implementing MBO is extensive.

Dr. Harvey is also the author of *Management by Objectives in Higher Education: A Guide to Implementation* and of numerous articles in professional journals and publications.

TABLE OF CONTENTS

TABLE OF TABLES

Chapter 1

INTRODUCTION AND DEFINITIONS

Management by Objectives (MBO) is a management technique which has in recent years been borrowed from the business world and adapted to education. This technique or system for administering a complex organization is sometimes called "managing by results" in the business community.

MBO is a simple logical concept which begins with the clear delineation of the mission, goals and objectives of an organization. The next steps in the process relate the activities of the organization to fulfilling the goals and objectives and to evaluating the organization on the basis of measurable outputs. The strength of the concept is in the quantification of objectives for the organization, as well as for the individual administrators and faculty. This process of quantification, if properly done, allows for a clear determination of institutional as well as individual performance. Full accountability is achieved and authority and responsibility allocated to the proper places within the institution.

MBO developed in the corporate world in the late 1930's and early 1940's. It has grown in popularity in recent years and is now used by most large corporations. Eight of the top ten corporations and two-thirds of all those listed in **Fortune** magazine's top five hundred corporations use MBO.

The popularity of MBO in education can be traced in part to the strong pressures on educators to be more effective and more accountable. Properly implemented, MBO provides a systematic way of organizing and operating a complex organization in the most effective manner.

MBO is particularly helpful to educators who become top-level administrators without proper preparation in administration or management. It is helpful because, when properly applied, the MBO system provides for the effective planning, organizing, directing, controlling and evaluation necessary for an organization to succeed. In short, to properly apply MBO, one is forced into doing those things which must be done by an administration if the organization or institution is to function properly.

MBO is particularly helpful in managing large complex organizations — in fact, it was the growing complexities of large corporations in the 1930's and 1940's which initially led to the development of the concept. As will be shown later, MBO allows for the proper distribution of work, authority, responsibility, and accountability.

The proper application of MBO allows administrators to get away from what is often called in business "the one-man profit center," that is, the president who is responsible and accountable for everything in an organization. This occurs when authority and responsibility are poorly defined in an organization, where jobs are loosely delineated, where goals and objectives are obscure, and where no one can clearly be held accountable. In this situation, all "the bucks" stop on the president's desk. He is the only one who is fully accountable.

Colleges and universities have their "one-man profit centers" also, which connote an inefficient and ineffective management process. MBO helps to clarify matters within the institution and to assign positions and responsibilities in such a way that all administrators become fully accountable "profit centers."

Before continuing, it is essential that certain basic terms be defined since some of the terms used in MBO have common usages as well as technical definitions. This is illustrated by the uses of the terms "goals" and "objectives." These terms are often used synonymously in common speech but they have separate specialized meanings in the MBO context. Even various systems of MBO use these terms differently. However, there is an evolving terminology and that which is defined here is consistent with it. A goal is a broad, timeless, usually unattainable statement which points to a desired end. It clarifies direction but is seldom fully attained. On the other hand, an objective by definition is quantifiable, set within a time frame, and must be attainable in order to qualify as an objective.

MBO itself has many different meanings. In the broad conceptual sense it applies to any attempts to use goals and objectives within an organization. In the more narrow sense and within the classical definition that is used in this publication, MBO is a management system in which, as a minimum, the institution sets goals and objectives for the total institution and sets consistent, correlated individual objectives for key personnel.

Some institutions develop only individual objectives for administrators, choosing not to develop objectives for faculty, programs, or other personnel. This form of MBO is properly called Administration by Objectives (ABO) since its use is limited to administrators.

Other institutions use MBO broadly throughout the organization. They will key off the institutional mission, goals, and objectives to set program goals and objectives, as well as objectives for administrators, faculty, and other college employees.

Later in this publication, various models for using MBO will be described and discussed which will further clarify the variety of applications possible with MBO.

One additional point needs to made here. Educators tend to react negatively to the term "management." It rubs some the wrong way and connotes autocracy and/or inappropriate (for education) business practices. Some failures in the education area resulting from the implementation of MBO have caused some to view MBO in negative terms. In order to avoid the stigma that is attached to the term in some educators' minds, some institutions are beginning to use different terms to label their MBO efforts. Terms such as Planning by Objectives, Administration by Objectives, Organizing by Objectives, Evaluating by Objectives, and others are being used. In one case known to the author, a college president avoids giving the system any label whatsoever to avoid the possible stigma. However, he is actively instituting the system.

In this publication we will use the term MBO and make no apologies for it. If some who wish to implement the system find the term to be a hindrance, it is recommended that it be called anything you wish or nothing at all. The important thing is that the principles and processes be accepted and effectively used.

The following are the definitions of terms that are used in this publication.

MBO Definitions

ADMINISTRATION BY OBJECTIVES (ABO). This constitutes a narrow use of MBO which involves using the system only with the administrators of a college or university. Individual objectives are developed for administrators based on the institutional goals and objectives. A broader based MBO would involve faculty, support staff, and program objectives in addition to the administrator objectives. This narrow use of MBO is easier to implement but seldom impacts on the educational program in a substantial way. Some colleges begin with ABO and broaden into a more fully developed MBO system as time and circumstances permit.

COMMUNITY SERVICE OBJECTIVE. This is an objective written to cover an administrator's activities in the community. For example, a college might require that each administrator be involved in a service club, the United Fund, or other community type activity each year. This category of objectives is the least used of the five defined in this section.

DATA BASE. This is a large bank of detailed data and information which can be accessed to meet many needs.

DATA BASE (COMPUTERIZED). This terms also includes a large bank of detailed data which can be accessed by other subsystems in a flexible way to meet many needs. It may — or may not — include data stored in random access information storage media. It normally includes (date stored in) carefully constructed formats for the storage of the *proper* data and provisions for the continual updating with current data. For the purposes of this definition, a data base, therefore, may normally be conceived of as being structured by files.

DEVELOPMENTAL GOALS AND OBJECTIVES. This is a category of organizational or programmatic goals and objectives. Developmental goals or objectives cause growth and bring about change in an organization as opposed to maintenance goals and objectives which preserve the status quo from year to year. Developmental goals and objectives tend to focus on innovative or problem solving tasks which cause organizational growth and development.

EDUCATIONAL IMPACT GOALS AND OBJECTIVES. This is a category of organizational or programmatic goals and objectives that deals with the impact of the educational process upon students. These statements relate to the types of changes or effects colleges hope to have on students and lead to a measurement of the education impact of a college on the student.

EDUCATIONAL PROGRAM GOALS OR OBJECTIVES. This category of organizational or programmatic goals and objectives deals with such activities as program and course offerings. In contrast with the Education Outcome Goals or Objectives, these goals and objectives deal more with process than with outcome.

GOAL. This term derives from the basic mission statement and is a statement of a single purpose which is a hoped-for accomplishment. A goal is broad and somewhat "motherhoodish," and usually is not quantifiable. It is timeless in that it usually has no specific date by which it is to be completed. A goal is a general statement from which specific objectives can be derived.

INNOVATIVE OBJECTIVE. This objective is aimed at developing a new idea or approach to some aspect of an administrator's work. To be classified as innovative, the objective need only be new to the area in which it is applied. It need not be creative in terms of state-wide or national spheres of recognition.

INSTRUCTION BY OBJECTIVES (IBO). This process teaches through the use of clearly stated quantifiable behavioral objectives.

MAINTENANCE GOALS OR OBJECTIVES. This is a category of organizational or programmatic goals and objectives which focuses on the routine ongoing functions of an organization. These goals and objectives outline the main functions of an organization or program. They are opposed to developmental goals and objectives which aim at the new, innovative, or problem solving aspects of an organization and bring about organizational change.

MANAGEMENT INFORMATION SYSTEM (MIS). This is an organized method of providing administrators and others in the management process with information needed for decisions, when it is needed, and in a form which aids understanding and stimulates action.

MANAGEMENT BY OBJECTIVES (MBO). MBO is a system of managing or administering an organization which places the major focus on fulfilling specific objectives and achieving specified results. In this system an organization clearly states its main goals and objectives. From these, each administrator or staff member derives concise quantifiable objectives which they agree to complete usually within a twelve-month time frame. The system focuses on planning, directing, and controlling for specified results. MBO differs from other older management systems in that it stresses objectives and results rather than activities and functions.

MANAGEMENT BY RESULTS. This is a synonym for MBO and ABO.

MISSION STATEMENT. This broad general statement is usually no more than a paragraph or two long and sets the parameters for an organization and summarizes the basic purposes for which an institution or program exists.

OBJECTIVE. An objective is a clear, concise, specific statement of one task to be accomplished in quantifiable terms. Objectives derive from mission statements and goals and lead to the accomplishment of these elements. An objective may be short-term (one year or less) or long-term (over a year, usually five or ten years). A good objective is quantifiable so that there can be no question whether or not it has been met within the specified time period.

OPERATIONAL OBJECTIVES. This category of institutional goals and objectives focuses on the methods or processes a college will use to carry out its activities. Such goals and objectives will deal with the management process, academic freedom, and other areas that relate to how an institution will function.

OUTCOME MEASURE. In the educational environment, this is a quantifiable measurement of the results or impact of an educational institution or one of its programs. It is a product of one or more of the educational processes. Outcome measures are designed to identify and collect information needed to determine institutional *effectiveness.*

PARTICIPATIVE MANAGEMENT. This management process emphasizes the democratic involvement of all people in the management system in the decision-making and policy formulation processes. It is humanistic in nature and is the opposite of an autocratic-dictatorial system. MBO, to be

effective in education, must use the democratic approach and be participative in nature.

**PME SYSTEM (PLANNING, MANAGEMENT, AND EVALUATION SYS-
TEM).** This is a term often used by the Federal Government and the
United States Office of Education. A PME System involves a *systematic*
approach to planning (both long-range and short-term), a systematic ap-
proach to management, and a formal evaluation system focusing on planned
outcomes. A *fully developed* MBO system fulfills the requirements of a
PME system when supported by an adequate Management Information
System (MIS).

PLANNING, PROGRAMMING, BUDGETING SYSTEM (PPBS). This is the
development of a budget by functional programs and the allocating of resources according to program objectives. Program budgets are usually made
one a one- and five-year basis and should have an evaluation component to
determine whether the program objectives are actually accomplished.

PRIORITIZED OBJECTIVE. In a complete MBO system, once objectives
have been developed a priority is attached vis-a-vis other objectives. This
aids in end-of-the-year evaluations, assignment of time allotted to completing objectives, and determining which objectives should be deleted if
new objectives must be added during the course of the year.

PROGRAM. This is the composition of all work and related supporting activities undertaken to achieve a *common set* of end objectives.

PROBLEM SOLVING OBJECTIVE. An objective which aims at the solution
to a specific problem. In MBO, these objectives change from year to year
as problems are successfully dealt with. They may aim at finding the cause
of a problem or at applying known solutions.

PROFESSIONAL DEVELOPMENT OBJECTIVE. This objective is aimed
at helping to stimulate professional growth in a staff member. As a result
of carrying out such an objective, a staff member should be a more knowledgeable and/or more productive member of the administrative team.

QUARTERLY REVIEW. In the MBO system, periodic reviews are required
between a manager and his subordinates. At these reviews (usually on a
quarterly basis) objectives are reviewed for progress and validity and an
opportunity is provided to delete or modify objectives if changing circumstances so warrant.

ROUTINE OBJECTIVE. An objective which relates to the routine or regular
duties of an administrator. These objectives are generally the same from
year to year and derive from the basic job description.

SYSTEMS APPROACH. This is a logical, rational procedure for designing a progression of interrelated components designed to function as a whole in achieving a predetermined objective(s). The methodology includes specification of objectives in measurable terms, development of possible approaches, selection of appropriate means to the achievement of the objectives, integration of approaches into an integrated system, and evaluation of the effectiveness of the system in attaining the objectives. MBO is an example of a system.

TRANSACTIONAL INFORMATION SYSTEM (TIS). A TIS is any set of established procedures for gathering and recalling information for use within the normal day-to-day operations of a major single line office (e.g., the budget office, admissions office, student records office, etc.) within the institution. The operations and functions of a transactional information system normally involve low or middle level management people who are concerned primarily with routine operations and daily decision-making processes — all within the perspective of a particular office's sphere of operations. The TIS contrasts with the MIS which synthesizes data from the TIS into reports useful to top management and Boards of Trustees for decision-making and policy formulation.

Chapter 2 discusses the systems approach to management describing how MBO fits into this conept and interfaces with PPBS, IBO, and MIS. The chapter further delineates the advantages of using the systems approach and how this technique meets individual and organizational needs.

SYSTEMS MANAGEMENT

MBO is a part of the systems approach to management. In the broad sense, MBO in education encompasses PPBS, IBO, and ABO. In these elements we have a series of subsystems all based on similar premises and working along comparable lines. In this chapter there will be a brief discussion of why the systems approach is needed in higher education and how the elements mentioned above link together.

Why does higher education need the systems approach and MBO to manage its affairs? The reasons are many but basically, as was mentioned in Chapter 1, they are the same reasons that led corporations to adopt the concept after World War II. Managing large, complex, rapidly changing organizations dictated that a new method be created to keep up and to compete effectively. Corporate officers found that the old "folk" or "one man profit center" style administration of the past (consisting of a strong father-like president who runs the total operation) no longer produced the desired results, and that trying to manage by controlling activities was no longer effective. Therefore, they moved to a system of managing by objectives, focusing on "outputs" or "outcomes" rather than on activities. They developed a management system that pushed much decision-making and accountability down to lower levels of the organization, where the action was "on the firing line."

There is another basic reason for applying the systems approach and that is that properly implemented, the systems approach keeps an organization focused on the quality of its outcomes. In education (and all public service organizations) we've sometimes lost sight of this fact, with unfortunate consequences.

One of the basic differences between business and industry (private sector) and education (public sector) is that in the private sector, the primary source of income comes from the sale of a product or service. If the product or service is not of quality, it does not sell and the corporation income is directly affected. In the public sector, the primary income comes from legislative appropriations or taxes which are only tangentially related to the quality of the outcomes (see Table 2.1).

If the private sector loses sight of the quality of their outcome, they usually fail in their competition with similar businesses and they go bankrupt. In the public sector, this forced emphasis on outcomes is not present. Educators can be inefficient, ineffective, ignore students and improvements of the educational enterprise, often with little or no consequence to their primary income. This is one of the major differences between the private and public sectors.

The other major difference is, of course, that the outcomes (products and services) in the private sector are more easily measured than are the outcomes in the public sector. This latter fact makes MBO more easily applicable to the private sector. However, the previous point (focus of outcomes, Table 2.1) makes MBO essential in the public sector. In short, MBO, properly applied, forces the public sector to stay focused on its outcomes and the effectiveness of its services. This has often been overlooked in the past. Priorities in higher education have often gotten mixed up and the quality of education has suffered. Society will no longer tolerate this problem.

There are other reasons why the systems approach is needed. They are:

- **Institutions of higher education are becoming increasingly complex and difficult to manage.** The old style of personal "folk" administration can no longer do the job. The "one-man profit center" concept is outdated.

- **Change is occurring at a faster rate.** It is difficult for top administrators to "keep up" and be experts in all areas. A new approach is needed that provides for expertise to be developed and used "on the firing line" where the problems and opportunities actually exist.

- **Educators are poor administrators.** Typically, educators are prepared as teachers, counselors, etc., not as administrators and managers. Even the graduate programs in the administration of higher education leave something to be desired in many institutions. The systems approach assists the poorly prepared administrator in organizing and managing a complex enterprise.

- **There is a depression in higher education.** The rapid growth of the 1960's and the dollar flow brought in washed out a lot of mistakes in planning and management. But now this growth is over and educators must get along with fewer dollars. The key to success will lie in the more efficient and effective use of the available dollars. The systems approach helps achieve this end.

- **The public has lost confidence in higher education.** A recent Harris poll showed that only 44% of the public said they have "a great deal of confidence" in the leadership in higher education. This confidence level had been as high as 72%. Educators must regain public confidence by being more effective.

- **A new level of accountability is needed.** Because of some of the factors mentioned above, educators are being called to a new level of accountability by their constituents — state legislators, citizens, etc. Table 2.2 shows how accountability is developed through using the systems approach.

In summary, the systems approach can help educators become more effective administrators of the education enterprise. It does so by helping administrators meet the needs of organizations (see Table 2.3), and the needs of the individuals who relate to them (see Table 2.4). Table 2.5 lists the needs generally met through proper application of the systems approach.

Chapter 3 develops a further definition of the MBO concept and the elements necessary to have an MBO system.

TABLE 2.1   11

DIFFERENCES IN FUNDING PRIVATE VERSUS PUBLIC SECTORS

PRIVATE SECTOR

(Business and Industry)

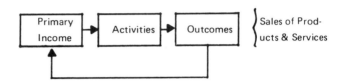

Income and Sale of Outcomes are Directly Related.

PUBLIC SECTOR

No Direct Relationship Between Outcomes and Primary Income.

Net Result is that Public Service Organizations (including Colleges and Universities) often fail to focus on the **quality** of their outcomes and organizational **effectiveness.**

L. James Harvey

12

TABLE 2.2

ACCOUNTABILITY IN HIGHER EDUCATION THROUGH MANAGEMENT BY OBJECTIVES (MBO)

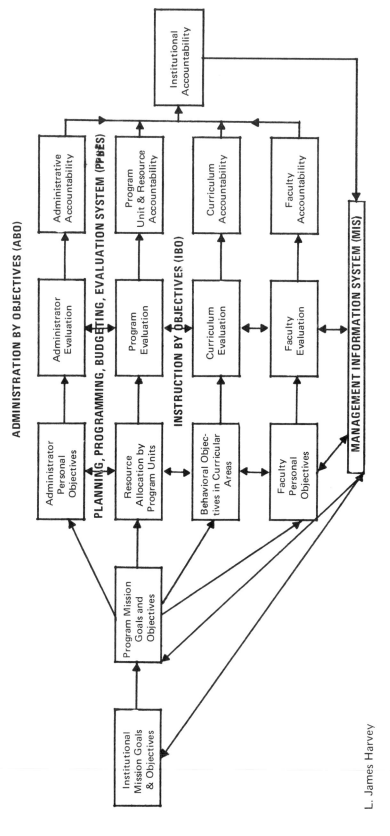

L. James Harvey

TABLE 2.3 13

ORGANIZATIONAL NEEDS

Experts in the field of management generally agree that the following elements must be present if an organization is to function properly:

1. *The needs of the individuals in and connected with an organization are satisfactorily met (see Table 2.4).*

2. *The organization's environment is free, open and growth-producing.*

3. *The total organization works together to attain clearly stated goals and objectives. All elements see how they are contributing to the total.*

4. *Communication is effective upwardly, downwardly, and laterally.*

5. *Openness and frankness characterize the interpersonal relationships.*

6. *The organization is structured around functional areas. The administrative and operational form is dictated by functional needs, not the reverse.*

7. *Decisions are made close to the action. The most knowledgeable people are the ones who make the decisions.*

8. *There are proper and well-used conflict resolution procedures (when needed) and little backbiting, empire building and power politics.*

9. *The organization is results-oriented and rewards those who produce.*

10. *The organization is flexible and can adapt to changes without precipitating major crises. The organization is not a prisoner of its own form and process.*

11. *There is a strong effort to facilitate human development and to help people, groups, organizational units, etc. grow and develop their capabilities.*

12. *New employees are effectively recruited, hired, developed and promoted on the basis of their abilities and accomplishments.*

INDIVIDUAL AND CONSTITUENT NEEDS

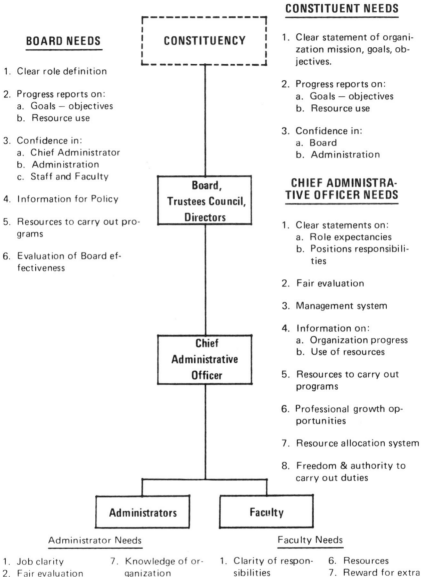

CONSTITUENT NEEDS

BOARD NEEDS

1. Clear role definition

2. Progress reports on:
   a. Goals — objectives
   b. Resource use

3. Confidence in:
   a. Chief Administrator
   b. Administration
   c. Staff and Faculty

4. Information for Policy

5. Resources to carry out programs

6. Evaluation of Board effectiveness

CONSTITUENCY

Board, Trustees Council, Directors

Chief Administrative Officer

CONSTITUENT NEEDS

1. Clear statement of organization mission, goals, objectives.

2. Progress reports on:
   a. Goals — objectives
   b. Resource use

3. Confidence in:
   a. Board
   b. Administration

CHIEF ADMINISTRATIVE OFFICER NEEDS

1. Clear statements on:
   a. Role expectancies
   b. Positions responsibilities

2. Fair evaluation

3. Management system

4. Information on:
   a. Organization progress
   b. Use of resources

5. Resources to carry out programs

6. Professional growth opportunities

7. Resource allocation system

8. Freedom & authority to carry out duties

Administrators

Faculty

Administrator Needs

1. Job clarity
2. Fair evaluation
3. Adequate supervision & guidance
4. Resources
5. Freedom to function
6. Management information
7. Knowledge of organization
8. Professional growth
9. Reward for extra effort
10. Understanding of role in organization

Faculty Needs

1. Clarity of responsibilities
2. Fair evaluation
3. Academic freedom
4. Professional growth
5. Knowledge of organization
6. Resources
7. Reward for extra effort
8. Understanding of role in organization

TABLE 2.5 15

NEEDS MET THROUGH MANAGEMENT BY OBJECTIVES

1. Organizational mission, goals and objectives are clarified.

2. Programs are related to goals and objectives.

3. The organization focuses on quantifying "outcomes" and evaluation.

4. Planning is built into the operation of the institution.

5. Resources are allocated more effectively and priority setting is easier.

6. Management information is systematically available in an organized and useful format.

7. Administrative effort is effectively focused on institutional goals and objectives. Wasted effort is reduced.

8. Administrators are objectively evaluated.

9. Information is available for reporting to the board and constituency.

10. Administrators have freedom to operate within clearly defined areas.

11. Organizational accountability is established.

12. Feedback is available at all levels of the organization.

13. Communication is facilitated and misunderstandings reduced.

14. Authority and accountability are delegated to lower levels of the organization in a systematic way.

WHAT IS MBO?

MBO is a much misused, abused, and misunderstood term. MBO is both a broad **concept** and a **system**. The two are often confused. MBO as a **concept** simply connotes the setting of goals and objectives, the determination of the best way of accomplishing them, and the evaluation of whether they are accomplished. Few people can argue with the value of the **concept.** It is not new and many people have practiced it for a long time. The concept is logical, practical, and hard to oppose.

The concept and the system which grows out of it assume the following to be true:

- *The clearer the idea one has of what one is trying to accomplish, the greater the chances of accomplishing it are.*

- *Progress can only be measured in terms of what one is trying to progress towards.*

- *Clear objectives for each program, unit, and individual within an institution provide the basis for establishing concise authority and accountability relationships.*

These elements are, like the MBO concept, difficult to argue against.

MBO as a management **system,** however, is another matter. While the concept is clear and acceptable, the problems develop when an attempt is made to place the **concepts** into a management **system** and apply it, particularly in education.

Following are the essential elements of an MBO system and an expansion on the definition found in Chapter 1. There are many shapes and forms to MBO. In fact, the form differs to an extent in every organization that uses it. However, certain elements are essential to every MBO system. Without them, an organization does not really have an MBO system. Basically then, MBO is:

- *A systematic way of organizing administrative work.*

- *An administrative tool which allows administrators to more effectively plan, organize, direct, control and evaluate their work.*

- *An extension of good logic and reason.*

- *A systems approach to administration which is also directly related to the Planning-Programming-Budgeting System (PPBS) and Instruction by Objectives (IBO).*

- *In its briefest form, MBO is an administrative method whereby an administrator and his subordinates identify areas of responsibility in which a person will work, set some standards for performance in quantifiable terms and measure the results against these standards within a specific time frame all within the context of the mission, goals and objectives of the organization.*

Necessary Elements in an MBO System

Unless the following elements are present, an institution really does not have an MBO system:

- *A clear statement of the goals and objectives of the organization.*

- *A specific program of administrator objectives within a specified time frame (usually twelve months).*

- *A periodic review of progress (usually quarterly).*

- *A final evaluation of the achievement of the objectives for the organization and the individual administrators.*

When first introduced to the MBO system, administrators frequently reflect on how simple and logical it is. They ask, "Why haven't we done this before?"

The answer, however, is elusive. In the broad sense, some educators have always used the concept. There have always been people who have managed their affairs by setting goals and objectives and measured their progress accordingly. It has been easier to do this in areas where the "outcomes" or products are easily quantifiable, such as in business where profits and products are measured or in athletics where wins and losses are easily counted.

In the narrow sense of the MBO definition, however, it has only been in recent years that a total system has been developed and applied to education. This MBO system goes beyond the goal and objective setting exercises of the past and develops a total process leading from the broad mission statement down to the specific quantifiable objectives which help accomplish the institution's mission. In short, MBO takes some old processes, procedures and methods and extends them into a meaningful new system. MBO as a system then, is a new process which has the potential for being far more useful than the previously used processes and techniques upon which it is based.

In order for the system to be workable in higher education, it must be used democratically. Subordinates must be involved in developing the whole MBO framework. If objectives are simply imposed on administrators and faculty from above and penalties assessed for not meeting them, the system will collapse.

One major principle to remember in applying the system is that **purpose** should flow downward in an organization and **method** should flow upward (see **Table 3.1**). The constituents, board, and president, with input from inside the institution, should determine the purpose and general direction. The administrative staff and faculty should determine the methods for achieving that purpose. This must be a democratic process with free communication, or it is in danger of failure. Participative management must be used in the application of MBO in higher education or it is doomed to fail.

A popular MBO debate topic centers around whether MBO is democratic or autocratic and whether it is by nature opposed to humanistic education and the creative arts. In and of itself, MBO is neither democratic, autocratic, nor harmful to any area of education. The concept, however, can be misused.

A dogmatic, dictatorial administrator can force unreasonable objectives on a subordinate and cause severe problems. This has happened in some places in business and industry. In order to succeed in education, MBO must be used carefully and with the full participation of subordinates. MBO can cripple efforts in humanistic education and the creative arts if unreasonable and inappropriate objectives and measurements are forcefully used. However, if properly used, MBO can do much to further efforts in these areas. (See Chapter 12 for a further development of this topic.)

Chapter 4 contains a discussion of the advantages and disadvantages of using MBO in an institution of higher education.

BASIC MBO PRINCIPLE

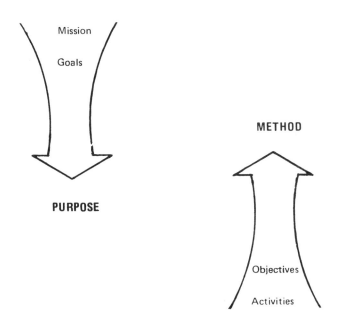

Purpose flows down. Method flows up. The administrators, faculty, and staff help shape the purpose but it is finally approved by the Board of Trustees. Once determined, the faculty, staff, and administrators should determine the most efficient and effective methods of accomplishing the purpose.

ADVANTAGES AND DISADVANTAGES OF MBO

If the MBO concept is properly developed and applied in an effective MBO system, the following advantages should accrue to the individual administrators (and faculty if they also use it) and to the institution. In addition, there are some disadvantages that need to be recognized and taken into account.

Advantages

The following advantages should accrue to administrators from proper application of an MBO system:

- **Clarified job responsibilities.** *In many institutions job descriptions are out-of-date and poorly written. Some tasks and areas of responsibility overlap others. Some that need to be delineated and assigned "fall in the cracks" and are not covered. Proper MBO procedures lead to a clear delineation of job areas. Tasks and objectives are specifically assigned and the administrator knows exactly what he or she is and is not responsible for doing.*

- **Greater freedom of operation.** *Because of the greater clarity and specification of job responsibilities and because of the development of quantifiable objectives, subordinate administrators can be given greater freedom of operation. Less supervision is needed because the parameters of their work and the accountability for accomplishing it have been clearly fixed.*

- **Better communication upward, downward and laterally.** *MBO builds in a communication system on significant matters. The setting of goals and objectives and the quarterly reviews help to structure meaningful dialogue between boss and subordinate as well as those in staff relationships.*

- **Greater satisfaction in work from observable results.** *The MBO system provides concrete feedback from the measurement of quantified objectives. This in turn provides the administrator with clear indications of how he is doing. Positive results give a far greater satisfaction from administrative work than is possible under the traditional administrative structure.*

- **Identification and remediation of weaknesses.** *The MBO system clearly identifies administrative weaknesses. This may cause some discomfort, but if properly handled, these weaknesses can be remediated and administrators can be strengthened. The adage that success springs from failure is applicable here. We strongly urge that institutions using MBO develop a professional development program such as that discussed in Chapter 12 to remediate and develop the professional staff.*

- **Fairer appraisal and evaluation.** *MBO allows for a more objective evaluation of administrators than ever before. Those who are really producing can be readily identified and those who should not be in administration can be weeded out. It also allows for the application of a merit pay or bonus system, as discussed in Chapter 13. In short, the individual administrator is dealt with more fairly and objectively than is possible under a traditional system.*

A number of advantages also accrue to the institution from using MBO:

- **Clarification of the institutional mission and a focusing of resources on appropriate goals.** *Application of MBO requires that the mission, goals, and objectives be clearly set and that they relate directly to each other. There is less chance that activities within an institution would be inappropriate or superfluous and wasteful. Resources in money, people, facilities and activities are focused on the goals and objectives of highest priority, reducing waste and inefficiency.*

- **Better basis for setting priorities.** *When goals and objectives are clearly spelled out they serve as a basis for priority setting. As educational funds become scarce, it is more necessary to be able to identify the highest priorities and allocate the institution's resources accordingly.*

- **Fairer wage program is possible.** *As mentioned earlier, a merit or bonus system becomes possible because of the base established through the objective evaluations. The institution no longer has to reward producers and non-producers with the same yearly increases. The motivation of hard-working administrators can be kindled and the resultant efforts rewarded.*

- **Better morale among the staff.** *MBO usually leads to better morale because of the increased communication and fairer appraisals, and because all administrators are carrying an equal load (if not, they are identified and dealt with effectively). In addition, each one knows what is expected of him.*

- **Increased communication.** *As mentioned earlier, there is an increase of communication on signficant issues throughout the organization. This aids morale and leads to greater understanding which in turn helps to develop a unified effort at achieving the institution's goals and objectives.*

- **Opportunity for new administrative structures.** *Because jobs are more clearly defined and accountability more effectively fixed, much of the traditional day-to-day supervision is unnecessary. This in turn makes it possible for an administrator to supervise more subordinates. The old span of control theory that one can properly supervise only four to six people is thrown out. This offers the possibility of developing some new administrative structures that can be more efficient and effective.*

- **Better planning.** *MBO builds planning into the operational framework and makes it a part of the ongoing administrative process. The once-a-decade development of a ten- or twenty-year plan which then goes on the shelf to gather dust is supplanted with action-oriented one- and five-year plans which are constantly updated.*

- **Management by exception rather than by crisis.** *MBO allows an institution to avoid many crises through proper planning and operation. It also allows administrators to function on their own unless exceptional situations develop. Instead of the crisis administration of many institutions, they can settle back, run more smoothly, and manage by exception.*

- **Improved administrative efficiency.** *MBO helps to avoid wasted motion and prevents the staff from engaging in superfluous activity which may be interesting to them but not valuable to the institution or focused on meeting institutional goals and objectives. Rewards are given for activity directly related to institutional progress, thereby increasing efficiency.*

- **Can save money.** *While this should not be the major reason for adopting MBO in higher education, it can be an important by-product of its installation. The greater efficiency and effectiveness that MBO produces can and should save money for the institution.*

Disadvantages

There are some disadvantages to using MBO:

- **It is difficult to quantify much of what we do in education.** *MBO is difficult to use if quantification is complex and hard to do. Measuring the "outputs" of education is only now receiving major national research attention. In many areas we are finding quantification difficult. However, we can quantify more than before, and as we build better data bases, MBO will become a more effective technique.*

- **MBO takes time, particularly in getting started.** *To get into an MBO system an institution must set aside some time to educate the staff, develop the necessary skills, and draw up the mission, goals, and objectives. Most institutions can find the time and in fact, probably cannot afford not to. The writer is reminded of the story of the woodcutter who was chopping at his wood with a dull axe. As he was cutting and sweating and not making much progress, a friend came by and asked the woodcutter why he didn't stop to sharpen his axe. The woodcutter responded that he couldn't because he didn't have time. MBO would sharpen the administrative efforts of institutions of higher education if they would take the time to implement it.*

- **Some arbitrary decisions need to be made.** *In the quantification of objectives, some arbitrary decisions must be made, particularly the first time around. Until a data base is built and experience with new measures is attained, arbitrary cut-off points are needed. Although this results in frustration for some, we must pass through this stage in order to establish measures which are meaningful.*

- **MBO can become a giant verbal game and paper shuffling exercise.** *On the whole, being intelligent, highly verbal, and inclined to use esoteric language, educators can easily distort MBO into a gigantic intellectual exercise producing high-sounding goals and objectives which are unrealistic and unmeasurable. The process can become a paper shuffling exercise with little practical value. The focus of MBO should stay on what it is trying to accomplish stated in clear, concise, quantifiable terms.*

- **MBO does not control ethics or morals.** *It is possible for an administrator to achieve his objectives while being unethical or harmful to others in the organization. This needs to be controlled outside the MBO system and can be done so. Chapter 13 includes some suggestions and an evaluation form which helps in this area.*

The advantages of MBO far outweigh the disadvantages. In fact, some of the disadvantages can be modified over time and by proper structuring and implementation. The next chapter discusses how to implement MBO and some of the problems that can develop in this area.

Chapter 5

IMPLEMENTING MBO

MBO is a simple and logical concept, yet implementing it is often a complex process. Many things can go wrong. Chapter 11 deals specifically with the kinds of problems that can develop. More than one institution has given up on MBO after attempting to implement it because they did not avoid some of the major pitfalls.

Below are listed some of the elements that need to be taken into account and the steps to be taken if successful implementation is to be achieved. In short, if you are considering implementing MBO, you should:

1. **Develop an implementation plan and strategy.** *Each institution is somewhat different and each situation requires a careful study before implementation is started. Tasks need to be defined and internal problems and opportunities taken into account. Some universities prefer to test the MBO concept in one college rather than to risk starting it on a university-wide basis. At any rate, a careful analysis needs to be made regarding readiness to proceed. As a result of this process, a time-phased plan of action outlining the tasks to be accomplished should be developed, such as that illustrated in Table 5.1. By all means avoid rushing into implementation without careful planning.*

2. **Develop a model for your institution.** *Chapter 6 deals with developing a model. It will suffice to say here that unless a model is clearly delineated, the whole process can soon bog down in the sands of ambiguity.*

3. **Clarify the program structure.** *This will be touched on in Chapter 6 for it is also a key element. Many colleges and universities are using the PPBS program structure as developed by the National Center for Higher Education Management Systems (NCHEMS) in Boulder, Colorado. If so, this program structure (PCS), or a modification of it, can be used to develop the MBO system (see Table 6.5). If PPBS is being properly implemented, program objectives have already been developed and should be used for developing administrator objectives. If an institution does not use the NCHEMS program structure, one must be delineated.*

4. **Educate the staff and develop skills.** *Before implementation can proceed, those who will use it need to be educated in the concept, in writing objectives, and in the quantification skills needed to use MBO. This can be accomplished through workshops, reading materials, and other means.*

5. **Clarify all job descriptions.** *Implementation is made much easier if all job descriptions are clear, concise and accurately reflective of the key responsibilities of each administrator. If these descriptions are not in good order, they should be reworked and cleaned up.*

6. **Review or develop the institutional mission, goals and objectives.** *Since the whole MBO process rests on this framework, it needs to be well formulated. Chapter 8 develops this area further.*

7. **Use expert consultant help.** *Make sure you have expert assistance in developing your MBO program. A consultant who is thoroughly familiar with the concept can give invaluable help in developing the implementing strategy and the model, educating the staff, critiquing the first set of objectives, etc. For so important an undertaking, the investment in consultant help is small and provides*
· *good insurance of success.*

8. **Obtain a staff commitment for implementation.** *In educational institutions where democracy is a cherished concept, it is important at some point to allow the staff to decide whether they support implementation of MBO. If they support it, full involvement can be expected. If they vote it down, implementation cannot be effectively accomplished without more education or personnel changes. The concept is susceptible to undermining and guerilla warfare if the staff does not support it and clearly see the benefits the system has for them.*

9. **Allow time for a trial and "debugging" period.** *It is recommended that at least one year be allowed for a trial period with the system in full operation before any evaluations or merit pay systems are tied to MBO. This will give the staff a "feel" for the concept and allow them to become comfortable with it. Early problems in quantification and objective writing can also be more easily overcome if a trial period is provided.*

10. **Allow enough time for proper implementation.** *In normal circumstances full implementation will take two to five years. The plan of action in* Table 5.1 *is a typical one. To rush the process faster than this is to court failure.*

11. Plan to develop a system of administrator evaluation with built-in rewards and punishments. *With its potential for an objective evaluation system, MBO provides an opportunity to develop a system of rewards and punishments which can effectively motivate administrators to greater accomplishments. This system can be developed democratically by the staff while MBO is being implemented. More is said about this in Chapter 13.*

In summary, MBO is a delicate concept to implement. It is more difficult to begin in higher education than in business and industry because of the greater freedom and democracy usually associated with higher education and the difficulty in quantifying educational outcomes. If the implementation strategy is not carefully developed and the matters discussed above are not taken into account, the implementation can easily fail as it has in several institutions.

The next chapter deals with developing an MBO model and presents some models currently being used in higher education.

TABLE 5.1

SAMPLE SCHEDULE FOR IMPLEMENTING ABO

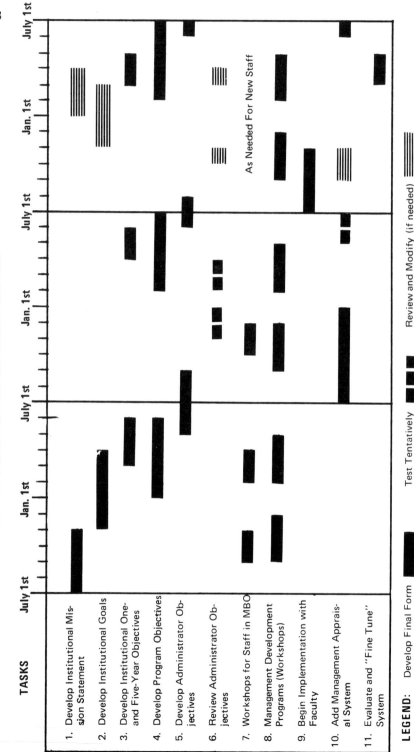

TASKS

July 1st   Jan. 1st   July 1st   Jan. 1st   July 1st   Jan. 1st   July 1st

1. Develop Institutional Mission Statement
2. Develop Institutional Goals
3. Develop Institutional One- and Five-Year Objectives
4. Develop Program Objectives
5. Develop Administrator Objectives
6. Review Administrator Objectives
7. Workshops for Staff in MBO
8. Management Development Programs (Workshops)
9. Begin Implementation with Faculty
10. Add Management Appraisal System
11. Evaluate and "Fine Tune" System

As Needed For New Staff

LEGEND: Develop Final Form   Test Tentatively   Review and Modify (if needed)

Chapter 6

DEVELOPING AN MBO MODEL

There are innumerable ways of structuring an MBO system. Variations on the basic theme can take many forms. If a college is to succeed with MBO, it is essential for it to clarify and develop its own MBO model. Without this structure chaos is likely to overtake the process. The actual form is less important than the fact that a structure or model is developed, communicated and understood by those in the institution.

By a model we mean a defined structure which makes it clear where goals and objectives will be written, and when these elements will be completed. In short, the total process of how this will be done needs to be laid out. In developing a model, the following questions need to be answered:

1. *Will we develop an institutional mission statement? If so, how will it be done? Who will be involved?*

2. *Will we develop institutional goals? Who will develop them? Who will adopt them?*

3. *Will we develop institutional objectives? Will they be regularly developed on a one- and five-year basis? Who will develop them? Who will approve them?*

4. *What will our program structure be? Will we develop program goals and objectives? If so, by whom? When? Will we use subprograms, or other subdivisions and will goals and objectives be developed for each area?*

5. *What form will administrator objectives take? Will the college specify the form for the objectives? When will they be done? Who will approve? How often will they be written? Will we evaluate and determine salaries on the basis of these objectives?*

6. *Will the faculty be involved? How and to what extent?*

As you can see, without clarifying the above items and others, some real difficulties can develop.

Table 6.1 shows a general model that is being used in higher education. **Tables 6.2** and **6.3** show two more specific models actually being used by colleges to implement MBO. **Table 6.4** shows a model being used in a large state community college system. Although the models themselves do not answer all the questions above, they do provide a basic framework. Further recommendations in this chapter on the program structure, in Chapter 8 on institutional goal setting, and in Chapter 9 on objective writing will clarify for the reader some of the decisions that need to be made and give recommendations on how to answer some of the above questions. Suggestions are also made as to some approaches that the author has found work best.

One of the elements creating most model development problems is the decision regarding the program structure. As discussed earlier, if an institution is on PPBS, the structure is already defined in most cases, because most institutions using this system also use the NCHEMS Program Classification Structure (PCS). **Table 6.5** gives an example of this structure. As you can see, the structure is complicated and has many levels. In building an MBO model, you must decide whether to write goals and objectives for each level. This could be a most time-consuming task. It is recommended that in the first year or two only **program** objectives be written and that the sub-program, program category levels, etc. not be used for writing goals and objectives. Later these can be added if desired when the system is operational.

Writing too many goals and objectives for too many areas will suffocate the MBO system and create a giant paper mill. To avoid this, the model needs to be simple and clear. The focus must be on the institutional goals and objectives and not unduly on the form and function of the MBO process. An institution rushing into MBO would be well advised to seek expert help in developing their model and planning their implementation strategy.

The next chapter deals with developing institutional mission, goals and objectives statements and presents some examples of these elements of the MBO model.

TABLE 6.1   31

A MODEL FOR THE MBO PROCESS IN HIGHER EDUCATION

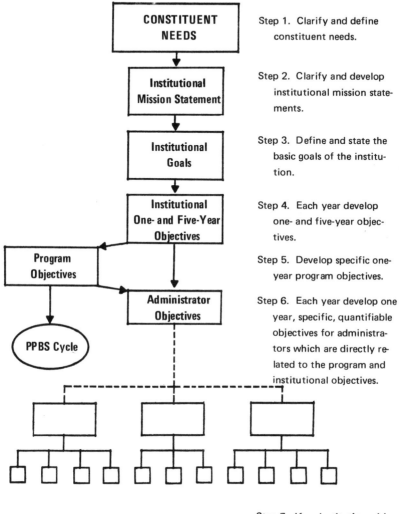

CONSTITUENT NEEDS — Step 1. Clarify and define constituent needs.

Institutional Mission Statement — Step 2. Clarify and develop institutional mission statements.

Institutional Goals — Step 3. Define and state the basic goals of the institution.

Institutional One- and Five-Year Objectives — Step 4. Each year develop one- and five-year objectives.

Program Objectives — Step 5. Develop specific one-year program objectives.

PPBS Cycle

Administrator Objectives — Step 6. Each year develop one year, specific, quantifiable objectives for administrators which are directly related to the program and institutional objectives.

FACULTY — Step 7. If an institution wishes, objectives can be developed as in Step 5 for department chairmen, faculty, and counselors in the same or a modified form of those used by administrators.

TABLE 6.2

SIMPLE COLLEGE MBO MODEL

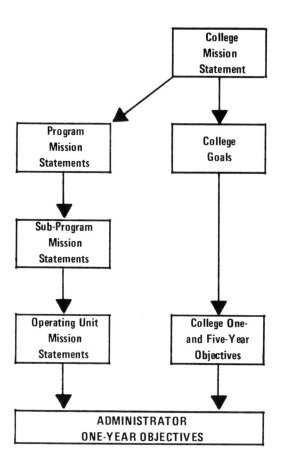

COMMENTS

This college has chosen not to develop program goals and objectives, but to relate these units through mission statements instead. Their program structure is made up of three elements (programs, sub-programs, and operating units). This model is a straightforward one that relates only to the administrators and does not involve the faculty or the instructional program in MBO other than through mission statements for academic program units.

33

TABLE 6.3

COMPLEX COLLEGE MBO MODEL

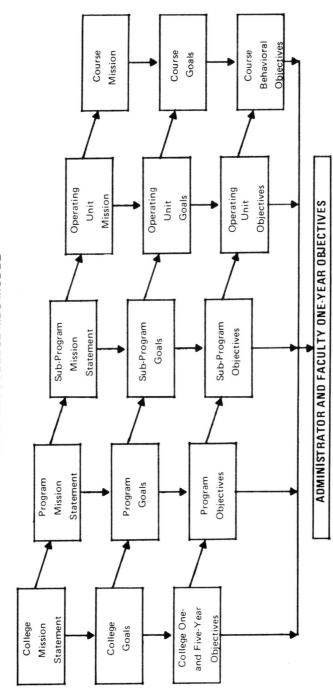

ADMINISTRATOR AND FACULTY ONE-YEAR OBJECTIVES

In the above model, mission, goals and objectives are written for all organizational units and tied into one-year objectives for each administrator and faculty member. The programs, sub-programs, operating units and courses are budget units in this system. The financial resources of the college are allocated according to program, and the objectives are evaluated thereby creating a modified Planning, Programming, Budgeting, and Evaluation System.

TABLE 6.4

STATE COMMUNITY COLLEGE SYSTEM (SCCS) MBO MODEL

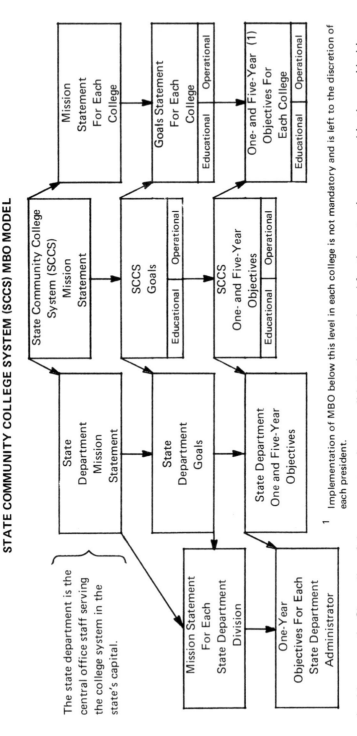

The state department is the central office staff serving the college system in the state's capital.

1 Implementation of MBO below this level in each college is not mandatory and is left to the discretion of each president.

In this system the Chancellor of the state system is responsible to the state board for the system's one-year objectives and holds each college president accountable for accomplishment of the one-year college objectives. The central office staff (state department) administrators all have one-year administrator objectives. College presidents have the option to use MBO below their levels in their colleges.

TABLE 6.5   35

LEVELS OF THE NCHEMS PROGRAM
CLASSIFICATION STRUCTURE (PCS)*

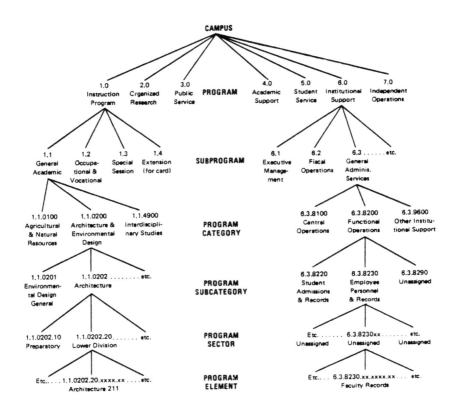

---

* The complete PCS can be secured from NCHEMS, P.O. Drawer P, Boulder, Colorado, 80302.

Chapter 7

QUANTIFYING EDUCATIONAL OUTCOMES

The heart and core of a good MBO system is the setting of quantifiable objectives. Without effective quantification, much of the value of MBO is lost.

Quantification is very difficult in education because measuring the end product of what is done, in most cases, involves attempting to measure the impact of educational activities on people. People are complex and many factors continually impact on them, making it difficult first of all to measure if change has occurred and, secondly, what factors caused the change.

Most readers will be familiar with the work that has been done to measure learning through behavioral objectives in the learning process. The psychomotor, cognitive, and affective domains should be familiar to most educators by now. If not, the reader may wish to review the work of Benjamin Bloom and Robert Mager (see Bibliography) in particular.

The writer will not review these works here. Much work has been done and much progress has been made. The psychomotor and cognitive areas are easier to measure than the affective, but much progress has been made in all areas.

This chapter focuses on quantifying the work of administrators and on measuring institutional outcomes.

Measurement has gone on in education from the beginning of time but the measurement has tended to focus on activities rather than outcomes. Educators are good at measuring the number of classes offered, number of credit hours taken, number of counseling sessions held, number of lectures offered, etc., but we have not often measured the impact of these activities on the students. The proper implementation of MBO pushes us to this more meaningful level of measurement.

Table 7.1 is an attempt to display the various forms of measurement contrasting the more valid with the less valid measures. Attempts should be made to move to the higher, more valid levels of measurement.

When beginning MBO, educators must often begin at the lower levels of measurement. Data bases need to be developed and more effective measures sought. This should not discourage those beginning to use MBO for the first time.

Often, activities are the only elements we can measure until we can fix valid measures on the outcomes. Frequently, descriptions and ratings need to be used until more sophisticated data can be developed.

Quantifying Administrative Work

Before plunging into quantification one needs to ask what it is that needs to be done. Usually, if the purpose is clear and the thought of an activity is clear, it can be measured. It is the judgement of the writer that many educators who insist that what they do cannot be measured are really unclear as to the specific objectives they are attempting to accomplish. If the clarity of purpose is there, measurement of some type is usually possible.

What kinds of activities do administrators carry out? They make budgets, control expenditures, supervise subordinates, promot professional growth in themselves and others, communicate, motivate, set objectives, organize activities, coordinate, evaluate results, schedule classes, etc. Can these be measured for effectiveness?

The answer is yes in most cases. For example, budgets can be examined for accuracy (number of mathematical errors, conformance to budget guidelines, timeliness of submission) and these elements can be quantified. Administrators can be rated by subordinates (and possibly peers) with regard to the effectiveness of their supervision and assistance to subordinates. In addition, administrators can be rated on a series of elements relating to their administrative work (see Chapter 13 on evaluating college administrators).

Much administrative work relates to time and time deadlines. These deadlines can be set and should be included in all administrator objectives.

Quality controls are more difficult to include in the measurement process but they should be included whenever possible. In many cases the work of an administrator will not have clear quality measures; therefore, the administrator's supervisor usually becomes the judge of whether it has been done well. For example, if an administrator sets an objective to develop a report on a subject by a certain time deadline, the objective has no quality control. The report could be good or bad and the objective is still met if it is on time. In cases like this the supervisor makes a judgement about the quality of the report.

Chapter 9 gives further information on writing individual objectives and provides examples with ideas for quantification.

Institutional Outcome Measures

Much work and research is being done on the measurement of institutional outcomes. The National Center for Higher Education Management Systems

(NCHEMS) in Boulder, Colorado has been particularly active in this very important area. Further developments and assistance can be expected for colleges and universities wishing to develop outcome measurement systems.

An outcome measure is defined as "a quantifiable measurement of the results or impact of an educational institution or one of its programs." There are two broad categories of outcome measures, the intended outcomes and the tacit outcomes. The intended outcomes are the impacts that grow out of the goals and objectives of an institution and focus on what the college is attempting to accomplish with students. Tacit outcomes are unintended "by-products." These are difficult to get at but they are important. For example, a college may, through the way it carries out its programs, develop in some students a hatred for writing. This dislike of writing is not intended and, therefore, it is a tacit outcome. It is obviously important for the college to know that this is happening, however, because it will have a negative effect on the student and his chances of success beyond college in most professional vocations. These tacit outcomes can best be sought through the student's feedback on the efforts of the college on them.

There are various ways of categorizing outcome measures. A recommended categorization based on the NCHEMS format is as follows:

1.00   Student Growth and Development
2.00   Faculty and Staff Development
3.00   Community Impact
4.00   New Knowledge and Art Forms

Appendix A includes a listing of one college's outcome measures based on the above classification system.

The intended outcomes of a college should grow out of their educational goals and objectives. Chapter 8 focuses on institutional goals and objectives and provides examples of some possible objectives with quantifiable measures. **Table 7.2** provides a listing of some possible outcome measures.

Further information on outcome measurements can be secured from the following sources:

- *The Western Interstate Commission for Higher Education (WICHE) has a project on outcome measurement as a part of its National Center for Higher Education Management Systems. It is working to develop measures of the outcomes of higher education and has produced several preliminary documents. The Ford Foundation supports this NCHEMS project. Contact: Sidney Micek, WICHE/ NCHEMS, Boulder, Colorado.*

- *The Federation of Regional Accrediting Commissions of Higher Education (FRACHE) has a three-year grant from the Danforth Foundation to study institutional evaluation with regard to accreditation. There will be an attempt to improve the use of institutional outcome assessments. Norman Burns at the North Central Association is the director of this project. Contact: Robert Kirkwood, FRACHE, One Dupont Circle, Washington, D.C. 20036.*

- *The Battelle Center for Improved Education, as part of its Project USHER, has for community colleges a cooperative program with the League for Innovation aimed at increasing the effectiveness of educational management. This program involves the development of both institutional goal setting and evaluation through management by objectives techniques. Contact: William Hitt, Battelle Foundation, Columbus, Ohio.*

- *Professor Robert Pace, of the Center for the Study of Evaluation at UCLA, has developed a Higher Education Measurement and Evaluation Kit to assess program and college effectiveness. It is intended primarily for four-year colleges. Field tests have been conducted and normative data produced. Contact: Robert Pace, Graduate School of Education, UCLA.*

- *The American Council on Education (ACE), through its Commission on Administrative Affairs, has proposed a program of studies designed to improve the resources for planning and management in higher education which would involve the council in a comprehensive project in the field of concern here. Contact: Lyle Lanier, ACE, One Dupont Circle, Washington, D.C. 20036.*

40

TABLE 7.1

MOST AND LEAST VALID MEASURES

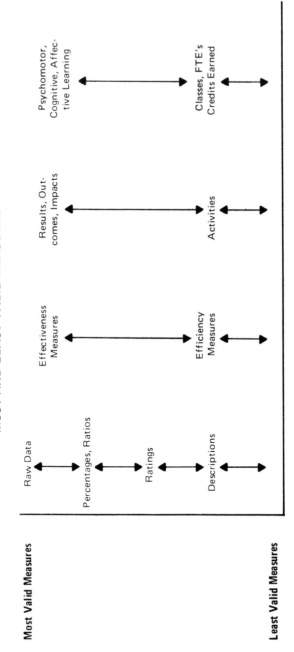

Attempts to quantify and measure educational progress should focus on moving from the lower, less valid measures to the higher, more valid levels of measurement.

L. James Harvey

TABLE 7.2 41

POSSIBLE INSTITUTIONAL OUTCOME MEASURES

1. Dropout rates by program.

2. Grade point average of students who transfer to other colleges.

3. Percent of students who seek and find employment in their area of preparation following completion of their program.

4. Employer ratings of students who are employed (3).

5. Percent of graduating students rating their education at the college as very good or excellent at one, five, and ten year intervals after graduation.

6. Percent of graduates who vote in local, state, and national elections.

7. Percent of graduates who are active in one or more civic groups one, five, and ten years after graduation.

8. Percentage of dropouts by program area.

9. Ratings of effectiveness of college by all students.

10. Research projects completed by the college each year.

11. New knowledge developed by the university.

12. Number of books and publications produced by the faculty each year.

13. Number of books and publications produced by former students of the college.

14. Salaries of graduates in various areas one, five, and ten years after graduation.

15. Percent of various population groups served by the college (age, sex, race, ethnic, religious groups, etc.).

16. Purchases by the colleges and dollar impact on local area.

17. Total salaries paid by the college.

Chapter 8

INSTITUTIONAL MISSION, GOALS AND OBJECTIVES SETTING

The whole MBO process rests on the precise definition of institutional direction. This is done in the MBO process through a clear delineation of the mission, goals and objectives. Examples of an institutional mission statement and
of goals and objectives are found in **Tables 8.1** and **8.2** and in **Appendices B**
and **C.**

The **mission statement** is a broad general statement of institutional purpose
which defines the parameters of the college's activities. This statement is similar to statements of purpose and philosophy found in many college catalogues.

The institutional **goals** are more specific and need careful attention. They are
subject to change and should be reviewed periodically at least every three years.
The institutional **objectives** are specific and quantifiable. A college may wish
to categorize its goals and objectives into educational program, educational
impact, and operational. **Table 8.2** gives an example of a college which has
developed its goals in these categories.

A major question that is always asked is who develops these statements of
institutional mission, goals and objectives. There are many ways to go about
it. Ultimately, of course, the board of trustees should approve these elements
since they set the course for the institution. However, the development prior
to submission to the board offers many possibilities.

For the mission and goals delineation, many institutions go to their constituents for valuable input. Generally, questionnaires are developed to solicit
constituent opinion. The Delphi Technique* is sometimes applied in order
to seek a consensus from a constituent group. Some commerical instruments
are also available. The Educational Testing Service in Princeton, New Jersey,
has an Institutional Goals Inventory (IGI) which can be used. For community colleges, the Battelle Center for Improved Education in Columbus, Ohio,
has a program which involves coming into a college district and polling the
various college groups regarding the desirable institutional goals.

---

* The Delphi Technique is a method for assessing group opinion and arriving at a
  consensus through a series of successive questionnaires (usually three) rather than
  through face-to-face group meetings. The technique was developed by the Rand
  Corporation. See the article by Cyphert and Gant in the bibliography for further
  information on the Delphi Technique.

Currently, much is being written and performed in this area of higher education. This approach offers a real opportunity for institutions to develop a meaningful process with many positive by-products from the wide involvement of college supporters.

Some colleges will not wish to undertake a broad study to review their mission and goals. In this case, current statements should be reviewed or developed by the administrative staff, faculty, and students. Task forces or committees and citizens advisory groups can be effectively used here and the products of the effort presented to the board of trustees for approval.

The institutional one- and five-year objectives should come from within the institutions. These elements are derived from the mission and goals and affect the means by which the institution is going to move toward achievement of its goals. Because the professionals on the campus should be the experts in deciding the means for accomplishing the goals, they should develop the objectives. The president should also play a major role, and when the process is completed, he should present these objectives to the board of trustees. After adoption, the board should then hold the president responsible for attaining the objectives.

In the MBO model proposed here, we suggest that the president's objectives be the institutional objectives. These in turn become an important element in the board's evaluation of the president's performance.

One caution: when a college decides to develop its own goals and objectives, it is not a good idea to use a set from another college as a model. This procedure can lead to an unwise emulation of goals and objectives which may not be appropriate. It may also remove the discipline needed to review in depth the college's own situation. Too many times in the past educators have copied and borrowed from each other and have lost institutional uniqueness and creativity in the process. In the case of the MBO process, we have found that the easiest way has not proven to be the best.

Setting goals and objectives, as was noted in the previous chapter, closely relates to the subject of measurement of outcomes. Colleges may wish to review lists of possible outcome measures such as those found in Appendix A to get ideas for the types of quantified outcomes possible for their use.

Some additional suggestions for writing institutional objectives are in order. The following criteria can be used to determine whether an objective is really an objective. Criteria numbers 1, 2, and 3 must be present. If a measure just cannot be developed, then criterion number 4 or 5 must be used.

Each objective should have:

1. **An Outcome:** *What is to be accomplished? What is to be achieved?*

2. **A Time:** *When will it be done? Date for completion.*

3. **A Measure:** *How much will be accomplished and how well? What quantity, quality, or cost measures are used?*

If number 3 cannot be included in the objective, then one or both of the following criteria should be added:

4. **An Action:** *How will it be done? What method used?*

5. **A Judge:** *Who will determine whether the objective is achieved? What method will be used to determine adequacy or accomplishment?*

The writer of objectives should try to:

1. *Avoid "motherhoodish" statements, oversimplifications, understated or overstated words, opinion subject to change, exaggerations, inexactness, idealistic terms, terms with a range of meanings.*

2. *Use precise terms, words that state how much, terms that can be proven, terms that can be quantified into percentages, ratios, numbers, correlations, averages, etc.*

Once institutional objectives have been determined, it is a good idea to assign priorities to them in order to clarify institutional emphasis as well as to afford a vehicle for modifying the objectives if circumstances dictate a revision of institutional effort in mid-year. A simple system can be used as follows: P-1 (first priority), P-2 (second priority), and P-3 (third priority).

It is also helpful to code the objectives to be sure that each one is related to a goal (or an institutional objective in the case of program, subprogram, or lower-level objectives). A simple system such as follows can be used:

Organizational Unit	Abbreviation Number of Goal or Objective
College Goal	(CG-7)
College Objective	(CO-4)
Program Goal	(PG-6)
Program Objective	(PO-8)
Sub-program Goal	(SG-1)
Sub-program Objective	(SO-6)

In this system, the initials of the organizational unit are used (e.g., CG for college goals, CO for college objective, etc.) and is followed by a number corresponding to the number of the goal or objectives in the college system. For example, the CG-7 above would refer to College Goal number 7, the CO-4 would refer to College Objective number 4, SG-1 would refer to sub-program goal number 1, etc.

For a further clarification of how this coding is used, see **Table 8.1.**

TABLE 8.1

SAMPLE MISSION, GOAL AND OBJECTIVE STATEMENTS

A. College Mission Statement.

The mission of Everbody's College is to provide a high quality, comprehensive community college program for the residents of Everybody's County. This program will include two full years of college transfer work, post-high school vocation, technical and career education up to two years in length, adult and continuing education, developmental education, general education, and a full program of student services, including counseling and guidance, to enhance and enrich the students' educational opportunities. Everybody's Community College will seek to carry out its program with the most progressive educational methods available as economically as possible, and with full accountability to its constituents.

B. College Goal Statements (List not intended to be complete).

1. Each Associate degree recipient will be a well-developed self-learner.
2. Each Bachelors degree recipient will be able to effectively use his leisure time.
3. Each Bachelors degree recipient will have command of a specialized body of knowledge and will be able to find work or be admitted to graduate school.
4. Each Associate in Applied Arts degree recipient will have command of a specialized body of knowledge and skills which will make him employable in this field.
5. Each Associate degree recipient will have the knowledge and skills to participate in our form of democratic government.
6. Each Associate degree recipient will have an understanding of how change affects his life and he will know how to adjust to change.
7. Each Bachelors degree recipient will be able to articulate a consistent philosophy of life.
8. The college will use the most modern management techniques in carrying out its affairs.
9. The college will use behavioral objectives and competency-based instruction in all courses.
10. Each student will understand human relationships and be able to use them effectively.
11. The highest priority in the college will be accorded to the education of students through the most effective means possible. Research activities will be subservient to the educational process.

C. Examples of Program Objectives (including examples of how to prioritize and codify objectives).

1. Instructional Program:

   a. By September, 1977, 75% of all college courses will be taught using be-
      havioral objectives.　　　(P-1)　　(CO-2)　　　　　(CG-9)
      　　　　　　　　　　　　　Priority　College Obj.　College Goal to which related

   b. By July, 1977, a foreign study program will be planned and readied for
      offering during the 1977-78 academic year. This program will offer col-
      lege credit.　　(P-2)　　　(CO-4)　　　　　(CG-8)
      　　　　　　Priority　　College Obj.　College Goal to which related

2. Student Personnel Services:

   a. By July 1, 1976, all counselors will be trained to offer human potential
      seminars.　　(P-1)　　　(CO-3)　　　(CG-7)

   b. By July 1, 1976, a new academic advisement system will be developed
      and proposed to the academic senate.　　(P-1)　　(CO-4)　　(CG-10)

D. Examples of Program Category Objectives.

1. Physical Education:

   a. Each student graduating in June, 1977, will have the knowledge and skills
      to participate in two sports with carry-over value to age sixty-five.

   b. Each student graduating in June, 1977, will have the knowledge and un-
      derstanding necessary to be an intelligent spectator in two professional
      sports.

2. Automotive Technology:

   a. Each two-year graduate in June, 1977, will be able to tear down, reas-
      semble, and repair a standard carburetor.

   b. Each two-year graduate in June, 1977, will be able to install new rings
      in any standard-sized American-made automobile.

3. Communications:

   a. Each graduate in June, 1977, will be able to read at the 50th percentile
      for grade 14 on a standardized reading test.

b. Each graduate in July, 1977, will be able to pass a college test on the use of the library.

c. Each graduate in July, 1977, will be able to use the medium of television for self-development as determined by a test developed by the communications department.

TABLE 8.2   49

SAMPLES OF ONE- AND FIVE-YEAR INSTITUTIONAL OBJECTIVES

A. One-Year Objectives (to be completed by July 1, 1977 unless otherwise stated).

1. The college will develop a revised affirmative action program and receive board approval by March 1, 1977.
2. The college will operate at a cost not to exceed $1,650 per full-time equated student.
3. The college endowment fund will be increased by 10 percent.
4. A study of the data processing needs will be made by an outside agency and a 10-year plan for this area will be approved by the president's council.
5. Twenty percent of the courses will be offered using the behavioral objective approach.
6. The college self-study will be completed and submitted to the North Central Association by April 1, 1977.
7. The college budget will be controlled to within one percent of the funded current operating budget.
8. The college will serve 2.2% of the population in its service area each year.

B. Five-Year Objectives (to be completed by July 1, 1982 unless otherwise stated).

1. The university will enroll between 13,500 and 14,000 FTE students.
2. The college will teach 90% of its courses using behavioral objectives.
3. The college will operate at a cost not to exceed $1,850 per FTE.
4. The college will add 10 new vocational-technical programs.
5. The college will have at least 50% of its students in vocational-technical programs.
6. The college student body, faculty, and staff will each contain a minimum of 15% membership from minority groups.
7. The college will serve 3.1% of the population in its service area each year.

Chapter 9

WRITING INDIVIDUAL OBJECTIVES

The writing of individual objectives is another key to making MBO work. This is where the "power" is applied to make the wheels go around. At this level personal commitments and accountability are established.

In the model presented earlier, all administrators below the president would develop one-year objectives and present them to the person to whom they report. Taken together, these objectives would be used to develop a consensus on the subordinate objectives for the next year. When the objectives are completed, they would be assigned a priority rating to help determine which should have major attention.

Once objectives are set and prioritized, they would become the parameters for the administrator's work for the next year. If properly written and quantified, they would become the focal point for full accountability. Competent administrators with clear objectives need little supervision unless something unforeseen happens. Thus, a management-by-exception situation would result.

Three times a year the administrator and his subordinates would convene for major reviews of the objectives. They would assess progress and make any needed adjustments in objectives due to changing or unforeseen circumstances. At the final year-end review, a final appraisal would be made of the administrator for that year.

The clear accountability and concise definition of an administrator's work means that less supervision would be needed. This in turn would allow for a supervisor to manage more people more effectively. The idea that the span of an administrator's control can cover only four to six people is no longer true. Under this system, an administrator could effectively have eight to ten people reporting to him. This allows educators to consider new administrative frameworks that have the potential for reducing typical administrative hierarchies and for saving money.

In the model proposed in Chapter 6, administrators would write objectives in five broad areas:

1. **Routine.** *The objectives derived from the job description. They are the routine duties of the position and are the same from year to year.*

2. **Problem Solving.** *Objectives that get at the solution of major problems in a certain area. We recommend that each administrator write two or three of these each year.*

3. **Innovative.** *These objectives aim at adding new elements to a program. Two or three of these should be involved in each administrator's objectives each year.*

4. **Professional Growth.** *These objectives aim at helping the administrator or faculty member grow professionally. Each should have several of these each year.*

5. **Community Services.** *Some colleges also require that administrators write community services objectives. These aim at involving the staff in community activities which will be beneficial to the person and the college.*

(Table 9.1 gives some examples of these five types of objectives.)

When writing objectives there are various forms that can be used. Table 9.2 illustrates three forms that are most often used. Experience shows that the **listing form** is the easiest for those writing objectives for the first time. It forces a discipline because the writer must declare what will be done to achieve the objective.

The **sentence form** is the shortest and tends to be used most often by those who are veteran objective writers. It is acceptable if the writer has skill in quantification and objective writing.

The **variable limits form** lends itself to greater quantification and more objective evaluation by the administrator by determining not only whether the objective has been achieved but also at what level. This type of objective lends itself to some exotic mathematical schemes, particularly where objectives are prioritized and numerically weighted. It is easy to come up with ratings of administrators vis-a-vis other administrators.

Table 9.3 provides some criteria that can easily be applied to objective statements to determine whether the objective is a good one. Tables 9.4 through 9.7 give some additional suggestions regarding writing objectives.

Prioritizing Objectives

Once objectives have been written by administrators, it is important for priorities to be assigned as is done with institutional objectives. This is done by using the same procedure as was described for organizational objectives in Chapter 8.

In short, each objective should be assigned a P-1 (highest priority), a P-2 (average priority), or a P-3 (lowest priority) and the P-1, P-2, or P-3 simply noted after the objective to indicate its priority level. The priority ranking is important in the final evaluation process and if work needs to be modified during the course of the year. In the latter case, if new objectives need to be added, low priority items can be deleted or postponed to a later time.

It is not necessary for administrators to code their objectives as is done with organizational objectives unless they or their superior feel it is desirable. If the college does not use program objectives, it becomes more necessary to code the administrator objectives. If coding is used, the same system for coding described in Chapter 8 can be used.

One point that needs to be covered is whether faculty should write objectives, and, if so, should they be like the administrators' objectives. Although the answer will depend on each college situation, the author believes that the first priority of faculty should be to develop behavioral objectives for their courses. However, there is no reason why faculty should not also write objectives in the same way as administrators that relate directly to their performance as faculty members. At some colleges faculty write these types of objectives with good results. Faculty objectives can certainly clarify responsibilities and provide to faculty members many of the same benefits that administrators receive.

Chapter 10 contains a discussion of what not to do if you wish to succeed in establishing a sound MBO system.

TABLE 9.1   53

EXAMPLES OF FIVE TYPES OF ADMINISTRATOR OBJECTIVES

Routine or Regular. I shall control the 1977-78 fiscal year budget for the Student Services area. This will accomplished if: (P-1)
Priority Number

1. *The total amount of money allocated for this fiscal year for the S.S. area is not exceeded.*
2. *All requisitions are correctly filled out and have correct budget codes.*
3. *No requisition is approved unless full funds are available to cover the purchase.*
4. *All transfers of funds are made through proper procedures and have the president's approval prior to being committed.*

Problem Solving. I shall study and propose a solution to the dropout problem in Math 253. This will be accomplished if: (P-2)
Priority Number

1. *All students dropping the course are interviewed for the reasons they left the course.*
2. *The instructor of the course is interviewed about the problem.*
3. *A report is written delineating the reasons for the dropouts.*
4. *A written report is submitted to the Dean of Instruction by June 1, 1976, listing ways of solving the problem.*

Innovative Objective. I shall institute an ABO system within the business office by July 1, 1977. This will be accomplished if: (P-1)

1. *All staff are oriented to the concept by January 1, 1977.*
2. *At least one Objective Writing Workshop is held by March 1, 1977.*
3. *All staff submit written objectives for their area for fiscal year 1978 by July 1, 1977.*
4. *A system of quarterly reviews is agreed upon.*

Professional Growth Objective. I shall submit one article for publication in a professional journal by July 1, 1977.   (P-3)

Community Service Objective. I shall be a member of and serve in one community organization during the 1977-78 college year. This will be achieved if: (P-3)

TABLE 9.1, Continued

1. *I obtain a membership in a community group.*
2. *I attend 80% of the meetings.*
3. *I present or have presented at least one program dealing with the college.*

TABLE 9.2   55

EXAMPLES OF THREE FORMS FOR WRITING OBJECTIVES

A. Listing Form. I will develop an in-service program for the student personnel staff for the 1977-78 college year. This will be achieved when:

1. *An assessment of the needs of the staff is accomplished.*

2. *At least four special programs or workshops are developed and held.*

3. *Each program receives at least a 2.5 group rating on a five-point scale.*

4. *The staff rates the overall program at least 2.75 on a five-point scale.*

B. Sentence Form. During the 1977-78 college year I will develop an in-service program for the student personnel staff based on assessed needs and receiving a participant rating of at least 2.75 on a five-point scale.

C. Variable Limits Form. I will develop an in-service program for the student personnel staff based on their assessed needs. The elements determining success are:

	Min. Level	Average	Max. Level
1. Programs or workshops	3	5	7
2. Rating per program (five-point scale)	2.0	2.5	3.0
3. Rating for total program (five-point scale)	2.5	2.85	3.2

TABLE 9.3

CRITERIA FOR MEASURING OBJECTIVES

The following criteria, when measured against each objective, will help determine whether the objective is sound. Criteria numbers 1, 2, 3, and 4 must be included, or it is questionable whether one has an objective at all. Criteria numbers 5 and 6 need not be stated in the objective, but 5 needs to be understood in all cases and 6 may be needed in special cases (see below).

Each objective should have:

1. *Outcome:* What is to be accomplished? What is to be achieved?
2. *Actor(s):* Who will do it? Who is accountable?
3. *Time:* When will it be done? Date for completion.
4. *Measure:* How much will be accomplished and how well? What quantity, quality, or cost measures are used?

The next two elements are optional. In an objective that requires a qualitative judgement be made in order to determine whether it has been met then a judge is essential. If none is stated, this usually is the supervisor of the person responsible for the objective. Regarding the action or plan this needs to be discussed and understood though it need not be stated. If criterion number 4 above cannot be met, then 6 is essential and 5 also may be necessary in the objective.

5. *Action:* How will it be done? What method used?
6. *Judge:* Who will determine whether the objective is achieved? What method will be used to determine adequacy or accomplishment?

The writer of objectives should try to:

1. Avoid "motherhoodish" statements, oversimplifications, understated or overstated words, opinion subject to change, exaggerations, inexactness, idealistic terms, terms with a range of meanings.

2. Use preeise terms, words that state how much, terms that can be proven, terms that can be quantified into percentages, ratios, numbers, correlations, averages, etc.

To be of any value, objectives must be quantified.

TABLE 9.4   57

CHARACTERISTICS OF GOOD OBJECTIVES

Good objectives should:

1. Be realistic and obtainable.

2. Cover only one issue or responsibility.

3. Be fair to subordinate administrators:

    Reasonable,
    Growth-causing,
    Not beyond job limits.

4. Be in written form.

5. Clearly fix accountability for completion of the task.

6. Involve only major job responsibilities or issues.

7. Express results to be attained in one or more of the following:

    Quantity,
    Quality,
    Time,
    Cost.

8. Cover only job factors which are controllable by the administrator.

9. Guarantee that measurement is possible by both the administrator and the person to whom he reports.

10. Carry a priority rating in relation to other objectives.

11. Be directly related to institutional and program objectives.

12. State if another administrator must play a joint role in accomplishing the objective including what he must do.

13. Be as short, clear, concise and understandable as possible.

14. Be a positive statement of what is to be accomplished.

15. Be realistic; resources must be available to accomplish objectives.

TABLE 9.5

OBJECTIVES MEASURE THESE FOUR THINGS

Quantity : 1. 1,200 students will be enrolled.
2. 3,000 new student applications will be processed.
3. Attendance will average 300 people per game.
4. Class size in composition will be limited to twenty-five.

Quality : 1. A greater percentage of students will rate their education excellent in 1977 than in 1976.
2. 10% more students will succeed at four-year colleges than in our last study.
3. The budget request will be 100% free of mathematical errors.
4. 95% of expenditure requests will have the correct budget account number.
5. No expenditure requests will be forwarded to the business office if they exceed budget allocations.

Time : 1. All budget requests will be in by February 1st.
2. All equipment purchases will be processed in five working days.
3. All new faculty appointments will be made to the president by June 1st.
4. The committee report will be made by November 1st.

Cost : 1. The cost per student will be reduced to $1,375 per FTES.
2. The student personnel area will expend $138 per FTES.
3. The teacher/student ratio will be twenty-two to one.
4. Administrative costs will not exceed 7% of the operating budget.

TABLE 9.6 59

EXAMPLES OF OBJECTIVES

Poor: Develop a good in-service program.

Better: Develop an in-service program which will have six sessions, at least four outside consultants; I will obtain a rating of four on a five-point scale from participants.

Poor: Do a fine job of developing my division's budget.

Better: I will submit my division's budget by the deadline date given by the business office, without mathematical errors, on the correct forms, within the budget guidelines and with 97% accuracy in using budget codes.

Poor: Develop a good lecture series for the college.

Better: I will develop a lecture series for the total college community involving at least five lectures per semester on varied topics with an average attendance of 300 per lecture. The series content will be based on a survey of student interests.

Poor: Improve the student registration system.

Better: All regular students will be registered within a three-day period and no student will spend more than two hours in the process unless the student develops a schedule conflict.

Poor: A staffing study will be made of other college counseling centers.

Better: A study will be made of six community college counseling centers in colleges similar in size and service areas to ours. Counselor ratio, hours worked, counseling philosophy, classified staff support, and student utilization of services will be compared.

Poor: High morale will be maintained among the classified staff.

Better: Absenteeism will be less than 5%, staff turnover will be less than 5%, and 85% of the staff will rate the job conditions as good or excellent on a year-end survey.

TABLE 9.7

COMMON ERRORS IN SETTING OBJECTIVES

1. The administrator does not relate the individual objectives to the mission, goals and objectives of the college and his particular area.

2. Objectives are set too low and thus do not interest the individuals in pursuing them.

3. Objectives are written about unimportant matters.

4. Feedback from past experience is not used to shape new objectives.

5. Objectives are unrealistic and unattainable; they are written to impress the boss.

6. No discussion is held regarding *how* the objectives are to be achieved.

7. When objectives involve more than one person this point is not noted and the tasks are not coordinated.

8. Objectives focus on activities rather than quantified outputs.

9. Objectives are too wordy and full of "academic garbage" designed to impress.

10. Objectives do not fully take into account obstacles which must be overcome.

11. Objectives fail to include new or creative approaches to educational problems.

HOW TO DESTROY MBO IN HIGHER EDUCATION

As mentioned earlier, MBO is difficult to implement properly; many things can go wrong. Some colleges have plunged into MBO too rapidly and without proper planning, and as a result, have experienced many difficulties. Some have even given up on implementing the concept. This need not happen if care is taken.

The following list of errors will surely destroy or cripple MBO if they are not taken into account:

1. **Assuming that MBO is incompatible with humanistic education.** *Accountability, quantifiable objectives and measuring outputs are anathema to some humanistic educators. They say these concepts destroy attempts to "be human" because the "affective" realm in which they work cannot be measured. Therefore, these educators reject all efforts to measure what they do. As noted below (No. 11), not everthing can be quantified, and it need not be in order for MBO to succeed. However, we can measure much of what we do and far more than we've ever attempted. MBO does not force measurement of elements that cannot be measured, but it does require a sometimes uncomfortable clarification of what it is we are supposed to be doing. This is a healthy approach which can help the humanistic educators by forcing them to focus more carefully on the outcomes they hope to achieve and the methods necessary to accomplish them. To say the MBO concept is opposed to the affective realm or to humanistic education is to create a false impression that can cripple implementation of the MBO system.*

2. **Considering MBO as a cure for all ills.** *Although it has tremendous potential for helping administrators and faculty to be more effective in planning and directing their activities, MBO will not cure poor human relationships, incompetency, campus power struggles, or other ills which plague some institutions. To assume that MBO is a cure for all ills is to heap upon it a burden it cannot carry. Unrealistic expectations will inevitably lead to failure.*

3. **Believing you are too busy to implement MBO.** *A number of college presidents have said they are too busy to devote time to*

beginning MBO. In most cases, they are too busy "putting out fires" and handling the very crises which could be avoided by developing a good MBO system. Extensive time commitments are not required to begin MBO. A week from each administrator each semester would be more than ample. The attitude that there is not time available to implement MBO will kill it in a hurry. Yet, administrators really cannot afford not to take the time, for they urgently need the more efficient operation that MBO can give them.

4. **Assuming that all is well and that MBO cannot help because you are already perfect.** *Some colleges fail to seriously consider MBO because they believe they already function at near-peak effectiveness. They believe the "folk" administration of the pre-1960's era is still possible in higher education. This may be true for a few small isolated liberal arts colleges, but for 95% of our modern colleges and universities a systems approach is needed to administer these complex and rapidly changing institutions. Remember, the Penn Central did not believe it needed the systems approach either — more than one person has drawn an uncomfortable analogy between higher education and this bankrupt corporation. In summary, a complacent attitude that all is well will inhibit any attempts at improvement and forestall efforts to implement MBO.*

5. **Trying to implement the concept overnight.** *Some colleges have been so attracted to the system that they have attempted to install it overnight. This simply cannot be done. In most institutions two to five years are necessary to fully implement MBO. Administrators need to be educated to the concept, objective writing skills developed, and institutional mission, goals and objectives statements reviewed and updated. The system should have a "dry run" period of at least a year before becoming fully operational.*

6. **Forcing unrealistic objectives on subordinates.** *This will kill MBO as fast as anything. Quantifiable objectives for each administrator should be set democratically and realistically. In the proper process administrator objectives are proposed by the subordinate to his superior. They are then jointly reviewed for relevancy and a consensus is developed. The forcing of unachievable objectives on a subordinate will lead to a discouragement and rebellion which can destroy the MBO system.*

7. **Creating a huge paper mill with MBO.** *There is always the danger that the value of the MBO system may be lost in a great paper shuffling exercise. Educators are usually very verbal and highly*

intelligent. Unless they maintain their focus on the objectives of what they are doing, they tend to produce a large number of esoteric pointless statements. The resulting paper mill would soon suffocate MBO.

8. **Emphasize the techniques of implementing MBO rather than focusing on the results of the institution.** *There is always the danger of becoming so caught up in forms, procedures, and techniques that we lose sight of the real mission of improving the educational process by achieving clearly stated objectives. MBO is a system that helps us more effectively establish priorities and focus on the outcomes of what we are doing. When the processes become the "tail that wags the dog," the system loses its effectiveness.*

9. **Ignoring feedback generated in the MBO process.** *Properly applied, the MBO process will generate a good deal of feedback on the effectiveness of programs, administrators, etc. If properly used, this information will help to improve the institution. If disregarded, a golden opportunity to become more effective is lost.*

10. **Omitting a program to improve, coach, and develop administrators.** *Some of the feedback mentioned above will relate to poor performance by some administrators. If this feedback is identified and analyzed, it will point to specific administrator weaknesses that need to be strengthened. Based on this information, the college should provide a program to help these administrators develop their skills. Moreover, a program should be provided to help all administrators develop professionally. Paradoxically, the educational field spends very little on the professional development of their managers while the business world sees the real values in education and spends large sums of money in this area. Educators need to focus more on this area, particularly since most educational administrators have been prepared as teachers, counselors, or researchers rather than as administrators. A professional development program is essential to educational survival as well as to an effective MBO program.*

11. **Trying to quantify everything.** *Trying to quantify the things which cannot be measured will destroy MBO. Although much more can be measured than we think, particularly involving the outputs of higher education, trying to measure everything will lead to discouragement and failure. For MBO to work effectively, we must quantify what we can and simply delineate and identify that which cannot be quantified.*

12. **Having objectives but no plans for implementation.** *To set objectives but not clearly delineate needed resources and plans for achieving them is to court failure. In requiring that objectives be realistic and achievable, MBO also requires that plans to achieve them be made at the same time.*

13. **Omitting periodic reviews.** *Once an administrator and his superior agree on a year's objectives, the subordinate is free to proceed on his own. It is essential, however, that periodic reviews (we recommend quarterly) take place. Their object is to report on progress, make needed adjustments due to changing conditions, and generally coordinate and communicate on important matters. Omission of the reviews destroys some of the value of MBO and increases the possibility of failure. Failure to carry out these reviews kills as many MBO systems as any other reason.*

14. **Refusing to delegate authority needed to carry out objectives.** *Once an administrator has his objectives, he needs the freedom and authority to carry then out. Refusing to delegate this authority causes administrators to become discouraged and to "pass the buck" for failures. This not only inhibits the proper functioning of MBO, it also deprives administrators of their initiative and creativity.*

15. **Failing to reward administrators who really produce.** *One of the advantages of MBO is that administrators are given the freedom and authority to produce quantifiable results. In an MBO system, administrators can be objectively evaluated and those who really produce can be identified. If these administrators are not rewarded in some way, their motivation will be severaly damaged. Not all educators are instrincally motivated to the point of continuing to work hard and produce results while colleagues fail to do so. We have regressed to a "low mean" too often in our efforts in education. MBO provides a chance to break this barrier and to reward on the basis of demonstrable results.*

16. **Focusing on MBO primarily as an evaluation system.** *MBO is a management system. Evaluation is a by-product. If a president implements MBO primarily to hold subordinates accountable and to evaluate them, the emphasis is in the wrong place and MBO will suffer. When subordinates believe the system is primarily an evaluation system they become fearful of it, play games with it, and generally subvert its main purpose as a management tool.*

17. **Refusal by the top administrative officer to change administrative style.** *For MBO to work, the top administrative officers have to modify their management style. They need to delegate more, to supervise differently, to plan differently, etc. If this person continues to operate in his old administrative style, then MBO tends to become an "add-on" which subordinates come to view negatively. The benefits that should accrue to the top administrator and the subordinates are usually lost and MBO dies.*

18. **Implementing MBO in an unhealthy environment.** *Implementing MBO puts a certain amount of stress on an organization — as all change does. An administrative structure needs to be in reasonable "health" in order to bear the stress and provide a cooperative environment in which MBO can flourish. If there are poor human relations, lack of cooperation, little teamwork, and other problems, then MBO will fail. These problems need to be taken care of first, then MBO can be started with a reasonable chance of success. To try to begin MBO in an "unhealthy" environment will likely destroy it before it can be implemented.*

Chapter 11

DOES MBO DESTROY HUMANNESS AND CREATIVITY?

The opponents of MBO in education usually criticize it for "lacking humanness" and for "inhibiting creativity." These criticisms deserve special focus in this publication.

First, let's look at the criticism regarding humanness. Webster's Dictionary defines humanness as a condition "marked by compassion, sympathy, or consideration for other human beings." Humanness is a condition of a person relating to other people. Let's see how this relates to MBO.

If MBO forces people to act inhumanely toward one another, then the critics have a point. If the system influences people to have less compassion and sympathy for colleagues in the administrative hierarchy and on the faculty, then the critics are correct.

Let's look at some facts. First, MBO is an inanimate management system with a wide variety of models and applications. It is neither humane nor inhumane in and of itself. It can be used either way. It is by nature neither democratic nor autocratic. An MBO system can be developed that forces objectives on people from the top down, that focuses on an organization to the exclusion of the employees, and that is rigid and unbending. This type of system would lack humanness.

On the other hand, there are MBO systems that are democratic in nature, that focus on participative management, and where human values are enhanced. In these systems, all employees are involved in setting organizational goals and objectives. They develop and propose their own objectives and negotiate them with their supervisor.

Some of the advantages that should accrue in a properly implemented democratic MBO system in education are improved communication, clarified job responsibilities, better feedback on work effort, fairer and more objective evaluation, and greater freedom to operate within more clearly defined boundaries. These benefits are hardly dehumanizing; in fact, they are the very opposite.

In short, humanness is a characteristic of a person. If a person acts inhumanely toward another, it is a matter of personal values and philosophy. The history of management and administration is full of people who were very humane in their conduct of administration and others who were very inhumane. MBO is an inanimate management system that can be used either way depending on the people who use it — particularly the top administrative officer.

The author believes very strongly that MBO — to work at all in higher education — must be used in a democratic-participative manner. If it is used in this
way, it promotes humanness rather than the opposite.

There is a related matter that the writer believes often gets tangled up in
this issue of humanness as well as that of creativity and that is the issue of
freedom.

Some educators may see MBO as restricting their freedom and, if it does so,
then they criticize it as being inhumane and detrimental. This could happen.
However, it may not be bad in some cases to restrict some freedom. One of the
leading university presidents recently said that "the American university is the
purest form of anarchy found anywhere in the world." MBO, properly implemented, does pressure an organization and its employees to justify everything
they do against the goals and objectives of the organization or institution. In
this context, some faculty and administrators who in the past have had unbridled
freedom and/or a laissez-faire operating framework will lose some freedom. They
are called to a new level of accountability as they must justify their activities in
accordance with the college or university objectives. In the judgement of the
writer, this is not a negative factor. Rather, it is positive and long overdue. Too
often, educators have followed their own selfish interests to the detriment of
the students they were hired to serve. In this context, MBO may be considered
negatively by the faculty and staff who lose some freedom, but the net result
will be a more humane educational system for the students because their needs
are more effectively met.

In summary, some educators may lose some freedom because of the need to relate all actitivies to the objectives of the organization; however, others gain
freedom because within the more clearly defined work responsibilities that
MBO produces, they are free to produce the desired results. The day-to-day
supervision is lessened and greater freedom within the clearly defined boundaries results.

This issue of freedom is a basic factor in the creativity issue also. Freedom is
necessary to creativity and if MBO restricts it then creativity is undermined.

The issue is really how much freedom and for what purpose. The writer does
not believe administrators or faculty should have unbridled freedom to the
point where the freedom is used for selfish or non-productive (in terms of the
students and institutional objectives) purposes. On the other hand, properly
applied, MBO encourages and promotes innovation as long as it is aimed at
enhancing the learning process and the organizational goals.

In writing objectives in the classical MBO model, administrators and faculty
are asked to include some innovative objectives each year. In this way, MBO
actually enhances and promotes creativity.

The only restriction MBO places on innovation is that it must be focused on furthering the purposes of the institution. This is a restriction the author believes is valid and necessary.

One last point, MBO as a system has some minimum procedures that must be followed. For example, objectives must be written, activities must be justified, quarterly reviews held, etc. Some see this as restrictive and inhibiting. On the other hand, when these things are done the benefits that accrue to the institution and to the staff far outweigh any restrictions that are imposed. MBO, properly applied, is certainly, in the author's judgement, an improvement on the way we have generally operated in education in the past.

In summary, MBO is neither humane nor inhumane, democratic nor autocratic by itself. It can be used either way depending on the values of those using it, particularly the top administrative officer. MBO restricts unbridled faculty and administrative freedom and forces those within the system to act to further the goals and objectives of the organization. This is good, and properly done it leads to greater educational efficiency and effectiveness. Within these boundaries, MBO promotes and encourages creativity and innovation and focuses these efforts on improving student learning, creating new knowledge, and/or bringing about social changes depending on the outcomes the institution of higher education has set.

Chapter 12

PROFESSIONAL DEVELOPMENT PROGRAM

A professional development program is an essential element in an effective MBO program. This program may have many facets, including individually developed administrator professional development plans, special reading materials, conferences, workshops, and advanced graduate training. One necessary facet, however, is an on-campus management development program made up of half- or full-day seminars and workshops on topics related to developing administrative knowledge and skills.

The MBO process will identify areas of administrative weakness which need to be strengthened. The management development program can do this. In addition, as mentioned before, most educators have not been prepared as administrators. They need the help of a professional development program in order to become good managers of the educational enterprise. Even those who have been well prepared can use a periodic refresher on key topics.

Business and industry can spend billions of dollars each year to upgrade and update their administrators. Can we in education who are committed by profession to personal growth do any less?

Table 12.1 lists a few of the possible topics for a professional development program. These programs should be ongoing on every college campus to help educators develop maximum effectiveness. They can be conducted at a relatively low cost, particularly if campus resources are used. Some consulting firms and universities have programs they can tailor to meet specific college needs.

Chapter 13 contains a discussion of administrator evaluation as well as a possible model for administrative evaluation based on MBO and containing a bonus pay system.

TABLE 12.1

POSSIBLE TOPICS FOR A PROFESSIONAL DEVELOPMENT PROGRAM

A development program for administrators is a must if efficiency and effectiveness are to increase. It is also an important addition to an MBO program because it allows an institution to aid administrators in remediating identified weaknesses and in building their administrative skills. In addition, such a program can be an invaluable aid in administrative team building.

Each college will need to tailor its own program to meet its unique needs; however, below are listed a few of the topics and objectives used at some colleges which have proven their value. They are presented here as examples of the kinds of programs that can be held.

TOPIC	OBJECTIVE
1. The Role of the Administrator	*To develop a clearer understanding of administration, its basic functions, the necessary skills of an administrator, and the principles and concepts of effective administration.*
2. Communication in Administration	*To develop an understanding of the basic principles of effective communication and their application in administration.*
3. Human Relations in Administration	*To study and delineate the basic principles of good human relationships and their application to administration.*
4. Delegation	*To understand and apply the basic principles of the delegation of authority and how it can and should be used for more effective administration.*
5. Personnel Selection	*To study the principles of selecting new employees and to develop procedures to be used in selecting personnel within the college.*
6. The Law and Higher Education	*To clarify legal issues relating to higher education as they pertain to administration and develop possible procedures to avoid legal entanglements.*
7. Coaching and Developing Subordinates	*To develop administrative skills in coaching and developing subordinate administrators.*

TOPIC	OBJECTIVE
8. Working Effectively with your Secretary	*To develop a more efficient working relationship between the administrator and his secretary by exploring ways in which they can more effectively work together.*
9. Management by Objectives	*To develop an understanding of the MBO concept and its application to higher education.*

Workshops can be built around these or any other topics that are considered valuable. It is suggested that they be concentrated into full-day or at least half-day sessions where administrators will not be interrupted. Off-campus meetings are more successful, but on-campus sessions can be productive if a secluded location can be found. It is better to bring in outside experts on the topics to be dealt with, although campus resources can be effectively and more cheaply used.

The overall planning of this program should be in the hands of a small, efficient committee of the administrative staff who will be participating. They should not only plan the program but coordinate and evaluate it as well.

EVALUATING COLLEGE AND UNIVERSITY ADMINISTRATORS

John Dewey, in his book, **Human Nature and Conduct,** wrote: "If education ever becomes a profession, educators may be held accountable for their actions." One can debate whether or not education has achieved the status of being a full-fledged profession, but, as was noted earlier, educators are being asked to be accountable as never before.

Some educators are still resisting accountability but this is a counter-productive tactic. Accountability is here to stay. While some legislators and others are doing some unfortunate things (e.g., line item control over institutional budgets) in the name of accountability, by and large, it is a valid concept and one that educators should welcome, for properly applied, it can only help us to carry out our work more effectively.

Unfortunately, most of the accountability pressures from state legislators and coordinating agencies focuses on efficiency, not effectiveness. The pressure is to do what we've been doing only at less cost. Few accountability efforts yet focus on effectiveness and quality. This type of emphasis is needed so we examine not only what the cost is of what we are doing but whether or not what we are doing is necessary, valuable, and producing the outcomes we desire.

Accountability, however, is basically an individual matter and it is closely tied to the evaluation of individual administrators, faculty, staff, etc. It is well known that you cannot hold a committee or task force accountable. You can, however, hold a president or dean accountable. When things go wrong, whether it be in sports or education, the manager and president get fired, not the team, board, or planning committee.

There is a great deal of unfairness in the way we have held administrators accountable in the past and our system of accountability and evaluation needs to be changed. This chapter is written to set forth some basic principles for administrator evaluation that undergird effective evaluation and tie into an MBO system.

Why Evaluate Administrators?

Before we evaluate, we need to ask: "Why are we evaluating?" It is in the answer to this question that we can evolve the principles for the system. We should evaluate administrators for several reasons, but basically it should be done to improve the educational enterprise. To help accomplish this, we should, in order to make each administrator more efficient and more effective in his or her work, evaluate them. More specifically, evaluation should focus on:

1. **Aiding in the professional growth of the administrator.** *Educators are often weak administrators. They are usually professionally prepared to teach or counsel rather than to administer a complex organization. Evaluation should help pinpoint areas that need strengthening so that they can become the focal point for professional growth experiences for the administrator. It is only after efforts to correct weaknesses have failed that an institution should consider removing the administrator from the position. This latter action is often avoided in education but it may be needed, particularly if the "Peter Principle"* applies to the administrator.*

2. **Identifying strengths in the administrator.** *An organization can profit from focusing on and fully utilizing the strengths of its administrators. These strengths can be used to "cross-fertilize" other administrators, to assist those with weaknesses, and to more effectively carry out the institution's work.*

3. **Providing feedback on work done.** *The literature in the field of pyschology on the value and need for feedback is clear and well-documented. We all need it, but educators seldom get it in any organized meaningful form in conjunction with their work. A good MBO system with an administrator evaluation system provides it.*

4. **Insuring that the administrator's work is making a meaningful contribution to the institution.** *Many institutions are loosely organized and more like loose confederations of programs and people than a tight organization where everything is directly related to the goals and objectives of the institution. Administrator evaluations should be tied to institutional goals and objectives to ensure that what is being done is tied meaningfully to the whole. More on this later.*

5. **Serving as a change agent for the institution.** *A good evaluation program ensures that the institution is moving forward and is changing to keep up with the times.*

These are the basic reasons why we should evaluate administrators. In addition, if we hope to evaluate faculty and staff members, the administrators should set the pace and set an example by having the best system they can devise.

---

* The "Peter Principle" holds that in many cases people are promoted in organizations until they are one level past their level of competency.

This chapter deals specifically with administrator evaluation; however, the principles and applications also apply to faculty and staff evaluations.

Why Have We Failed in the Past?

Past evaluations of administrators have not been very effective for the following reasons:

1. *They have been too subjective. They haven't been based on clear-cut objective and quantifiable expectancies.*

2. *They have often been based on character traits rather than clear-cut quantifiable outcomes.*

3. *They have frequently been based in part on poorly written and poorly thought-out job descriptions which are only loosely, if at all, related to the institutional goals and objectives.*

4. *They often only involved an administrator's immediate superior and ignored important input from others inside and outside of the institution.*

5. *They often focused more on effort expended rather than results produced.*

6. *They have not related the administrator's work to the goals, objectives and priorities of the total institution.*

It is only in overcoming these problems that we can begin to develop an evaluation system that will effectively serve the educational enterprise as well as the individual administrator.

What are the Principles Behind a Good Evaluation System?

An effective administrative evaluation system will embrace the following principles:

1. *It will be as objective as possible, focusing on quantifiable objectives agreed upon well in advance of the final evaluation.*

2. *It will focus on outcomes rather than activities.*

3. *It will relate the administrator's objectives and priorities to the goals, objectives, and priorities of the institution.*

4. It will focus on the growth and development of the administrator and will not be principally punitive in nature.

5. It will involve information from subordinates, peers, and others who have valid input into the evaluation.

6. It will provide at least one level of appeal without prejudice should an administrator feel he has been unfairly evaluated.

7. It will be tied to a reward and punishment system.

Having stated the basic principles, it is now appropriate to outline an evaluation system model which combines the above principles. The system discussed below is based on the MBO model presented earlier. As was noted there, MBO is basically a management system and evaluation is a "by-product." MBO provides the opportunity to tie effective evaluation to the system but it should be done carefully and only after the MBO system has been implemented and the administrators feel comfortable using it to administer the institution's affairs.

Design for an Effective Evaluation System

The following administrative evaluation system makes certain assumptions about the college using it. If the assumptions are not true, then the system cannot fully function.

The first assumption is that the college has clearly stated its missions and goals and has laid out specific quantifiable one-year objectives. It is also assumed that each administrator has clear, concise objectives defined and approved by a supervisor.

In this evaluation system, we recommend that the President of the college be held accountable by the Board of Trustees for achieving the one-year objectives of the college. Below the president, each administrator would be accountable for their one-year objectives which are tied and coded directly to the goals and objectives of the institution. These objectives are negotiated with the administrator's superior before the year begins and become the major point of the evaluation system. The administrator and his superior review them quarterly and have a final evaluation session at the end of the year.

Before the year begins, the two administrators also agree on which peers and subordinates (also students, faculty, or staff) will be asked to rate the administrator on his or her efficiency and effectiveness at the end of the academic year. A more traditional rating sheet can be designed to gather this data. A simple rating sheet with a Likert-type scale rating pertinent questions and characteristics will provide this element of the evaluation system. A sample of such a rating instrument is found in **Table** 13.2.

This evaluation system assumes that once the objectives have been negotiated and agreed upon, they will be reviewed at least quarterly. At the end of the year a final evaluation session is held between the administrator and the person to whom he reports. The data from the rating sheet is available as well as the knowledge of what percent of the administrator's objectives were accomplished.

In this system, the two administrators work to develop a consensus on the subordinate's placement in Line A (see **Table 13.1**). This placement is based on the percent of objectives achieved (Line B), which should be about 80% of the total evaluation, plus the rating sheet (Line C). (This line assumes a Likert-type rating of 1-10 on administrative characteristics similar to that found in Table 13.2.) The rating sheet is about 20% of the total evaluation. In the rare event that a consensus cannot be reached, the administrator's superior makes the final decision.

Once the administrator's rating is determined, the bonus system would work as follows. Each year the college would determine what percentages would apply in Line D. Generally, the middle of the scale would be at about the cost-of-living increase or the average faculty increase for that year. This mid-point figure is important because it determines the bonus structure. In the example in Table 13.1, 5.5% is the mid-point (Line D). All administrators receiving a rating at or above the mid-point, thereby falling in Boxes 6 through 10 (Line A), would have the 5.5% added to their base salary for the next year and the remainder (difference between 5.5.% and total percentage) paid by a single year-end bonus check. Those rated in Boxes 2 through 5 would receive the percentage attached to that box added to their base salary. Anyone in Box 1 would receive no salary increase and would be notified that unless significant improvement took place by the middle of the next academic year, they would be replaced. Those in Boxes 2 and 3 would be told that they need to improve performance, and a plan of action would be developed to help them. If improvement were not evident at the end of the next year, they would also be replaced.

To clarify, let us take an example. Assume an administrator and his superior, based on the objectives and rating scale figures, agree the administrator should be in Box 8. If the administrator's current salary is $20,000 a year, it would be raised to $21,000 for the next year ($20,000 + 5.5%) and the administrator would receive a bonus check of $500 ($20,000 x 2.5%, Line E).

For administrators who fall below Box 6 and get a salary increase below 5.5%, the difference between their salary increase and the 5.5% would be restored to their base salary during the next year if their evaluation rating for that year improves to Box 6 or better. In effect, anyone receiving less than a cost-of-living increase can have his purchasing power restored to the base salary the next year through improved performance.

While this system has its flaws, it does provide a way to begin to reward the administrators who produce and to warn those who do not.

This administrator evaluation system is one example of a system which can be tied to MBO. Other models and variations on this model are also possible.

Educational systems that cannot give bonuses or merit pay raises may still wish to evaluate, as described in this chapter, primarily for professional development purposes. In addition, non-monetary awards could be given such as public recognition, professional development opportunities (trips, books, leaves, etc.), promotions, or multi-year contracts.

TABLE 13.1

ADMINISTRATOR EVALUATION AND BONUS SYSTEM

LINE A Total Rating Line B (75-85%) + Line C (15-25%)	1	2	3	4	5	6	7	8	9	10
	Unsatisfactory		Needs Improvement		Average		Above Average		Outstanding	
LINE B % of Objectives Completed	65% or less		65-75%		75-80%		85-95%		96-100%	
LINE C Rating Scale Average Table	7 or more		6-7		5-6		3-4		1-2	
LINE D Salary Increase	0%	2%	3%	4%	5%	5.5%*	5.5%	5.5%	5.5%	5.5%
LINE E Bonus	0%	0%	0%	0%	0%	.5%	1.5%	2.5%	3.5%	4.5%

*Cost-of-living increase or average faculty increase.

TABLE 13.2   79

ADMINISTRATIVE RATING SCALE

Administrator
Being Rated _____

Please rate the administrator named above on the characteristics below. Place the appropriate number (from 1 to 10, or X or 0) of your rating on the line preceding the characteristic.

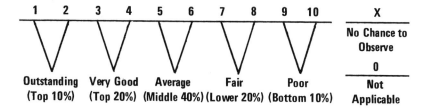

1 2	3 4	5 6	7 8	9 10	X
Outstanding	Very Good	Average	Fair	Poor	No Chance to Observe
(Top 10%)	(Top 20%)	(Middle 40%)	(Lower 20%)	(Bottom 10%)	0
					Not Applicable

CHARACTERISTICS

_____ 1. **Institutional Mission.** Knowledge of the mission, goals and objectives of the college and willingness to weigh decisions in light of the total institutional good.

_____ 2. **Specific Knowledge.** Technical knowledge and skill for the area of specific responsibility assigned. Is the person competent, experienced, well informed, and keeping abreast of developments in his/her area?

_____ 3. **Emotional Stability.** Does the person maintain an emotional balance, keeping his/her "cool" in difficult circumstances? Is he/she able to keep emotions from unduly affecting decisions? Is he/she emotionally healthy?

_____ 4. **Human Relationships.** Does the person use tact and diplomacy in human relationships? Is he/she able to handle disagreements with finesse? Does he/she deal with others in a spirit of love and sincere concern? (Is he/she basically self-centered and seeking to further personal goals at the expense of others, or is he/she honestly concerned with those with whom he/she works?)

_____ 5. **Democratic Processes.** Knowledge and skill in using democratic processes when appropriate. Does the person recognize and accept rights of others to participate in making decisions? Does he/she accept their judgements although different from his/hers? Is he/she convinced of the value of the "collective mind" vs. one man's opinion?

_____ **6. Personal Integrity.** Does the person deal with others with honesty and openness? Is he/she truthful? Can he/she be trusted?

_____ **7. Work Level.** Ability and willingness to dig in and work hard, to put in extra hours if needed, willingness to do difficult tasks, to do extra work, to take work home or come back to office on "off-hours." Thinks of work to be done and does it rather than "watches the clock."

_____ **8. Organization.** Ability to organize area of responsibility and tasks so that work is done with a maximum of efficiency. Ability to expedite work and accomplish objectives effectively through good organizational procedures and structure.

_____ **9. Creativeness.** Ability to perceive and use new or creative approaches in work, and willingness to try new ideas and concepts. Is the person flexible? Committed to change?

_____ **10. Problem Solving.** Ability to use good problem solving technique. Is the person logical? Does he/she study all alternatives, collect facts thoroughly and study results of previous decisions? Does he/she use scientific methods in solving problems?

_____ **11. Morale Maintenance.** Does the administrator work effectively to maintain a high morale among subordinates and between himself/ herself, his/her staff, and others within the institution? Does he/ she help avoid personality conflicts, backbiting, criticism of others on staff or in college? Is there a feeling of friendliness, sense of teamwork, feeling of importance in total picture of institutional effort?

_____ **12. Personal Appearance.** Does the person maintain high standards of personal appearance? Does he/she dress well and appear well groomed? Are his/her clothes stylish and in good taste? Is his/ her appearance in keeping with contemporary community standards for a professional person?

_____ **13. Objectivity.** Is the person able to keep emotion from distorting his/her perspective? Can he/she look at problems with clarity, logic, and coolness and make decisions on basis of facts?

_____ **14. Administrative Protocol.** Awareness of the administrative structure and willingness to work within it. Does the person respect lines of authority and staff relationships? Are decisions made appropriately and communicated to appropriate offices?

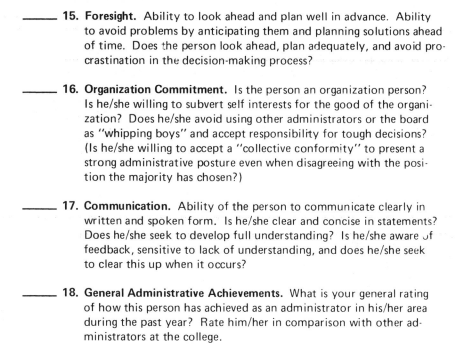

_____ **15. Foresight.** Ability to look ahead and plan well in advance. Ability to avoid problems by anticipating them and planning solutions ahead of time. Does the person look ahead, plan adequately, and avoid procrastination in the decision-making process?

_____ **16. Organization Commitment.** Is the person an organization person? Is he/she willing to subvert self interests for the good of the organization? Does he/she avoid using other administrators or the board as "whipping boys" and accept responsibility for tough decisions? (Is he/she willing to accept a "collective conformity" to present a strong administrative posture even when disagreeing with the position the majority has chosen?)

_____ **17. Communication.** Ability of the person to communicate clearly in written and spoken form. Is he/she clear and concise in statements? Does he/she seek to develop full understanding? Is he/she aware of feedback, sensitive to lack of understanding, and does he/she seek to clear this up when it occurs?

_____ **18. General Administrative Achievements.** What is your general rating of how this person has achieved as an administrator in his/her area during the past year? Rate him/her in comparison with other administrators at the college.

Chapter 14

QUESTIONS MOST ASKED ABOUT MBO

After years of experience in implementing MBO and conducting many work-shops, certain questions are repeatedly asked. This section contains these most asked questions and the author's responses to them.

1. **Can MBO be implemented in one department, division, or unit of an institution if the whole institution is not on the system?**

   The answer is yes. MBO has value in any size unit or organization and can be used with benefit even by individuals. Greater benefits accrue if the total organization is on MBO. If the total organiza-tion is not on MBO, then the interface with organizational goals and objectives can be made only by assumption. Thus, some of the coordination, priority setting, and harmonization of effort is lost.

2. **Doesn't MBO kill creativity and put people in "boxes"?**

   The answer is no if MBO is used correctly. See Chapter 11 for a fuller discussion of this issue.

3. **Is it necessary to quantify everything for MBO to work?**

   No. The more quantifiable outcomes that can be used the better. Where outcomes cannot be found, quantify and describe the ac-tivities that will be carried out. The outcomes in these cases should be described even though their accomplishment is assumed and not measured, particularly in the early stages of using MBO. Quantification is difficult; nevertheless, MBO has value and can be effectively used.

4. **Since MBO comes from the business world where outcomes are easily measured, can it be used in education where the measure-ment of the outcomes is very difficult?**

   MBO can be used effectively if it is modified to suit the educa-tional environment. If participative management is used, if the democratic processes are used, if delegation is properly used and administrators gain greater freedom, and if the quantification and objective writing are taken seriously, then it can work. Elements

*that cannot be quantified can be described in detail in terms of ex-
pected outcomes and left at that point.*

5. **Name some colleges and universities who are successfully using MBO.**

*The most successful is probably William Rainey Harper College in
Illinois. They were one of the first to use it and have been successful with it for over seven years. Others among the community colleges are Joliet Junior College in Illinois, Kalamazoo Valley Community College in Michigan, and Howard Community College in
Maryland. Among universities, Brigham Young University, the
University of Tennessee, and Utah State University are using MBO
in total or in part. One state community college system (Virginia)
is currently implementing the concept. This is the only state system known to the author to be using the MBO system. Several
state systems use PPBS, but do not combine it with MBO.*

6. **How much time per year must administrators spend in order to
successfully implement MBO?**

*The first year takes the most time; however, even then it is not an
inordinate amount of time. If an administrator can find time to
attend three or four full-day workshops, and, in addition, find
about one and one-half weeks of time spread out over the year to
write and review objectives, then there is time available to implement MBO. In succeeding years, the time to keep it going is
about the same. Proper implementation should save the administrators at least two to three times the time expended in starting
and monitoring the system.*

7. **How does MBO relate to the budget?**

*There must be a direct relationship because without funds, ob-
jectives cannot be accomplished. The relationship to the budget,
however, can be a close and tight one as, for example, you have
when PPBS is used with MBO (see Table 2.2 in Chapter 2), or it
can be a looser relationship where each administrator is left to
budget and make judgements about whether or not funds exist
to carry out the objectives.*

8. **Does a college need a director of MBO to implement and ensure
success of the system?**

*No. In fact, to have such a person would seriously damage MBO.
The key to MBO's success is to have every manager from the president (or Board of Trustees) on down committed to using the*

*system and to carrying out their "piece of the action." The presi-
dent must support MBO and do what is necessary to ensure that
the planning is done, objectives set, quarterly reviews carried out,
evaluations made, feedback used, and other elements such as a
professional development program carried out in order to make
MBO go.*

10. **What kinds of services can a consultant provide in implementing
     MBO?**

    *Consultants can be effective in providing the following services:
    (1) needs assessment and readiness evaluation, (2) developing
    models and MBO guides, (3) carrying out introductory and skills
    workshops, (4) critiquing the first set of objectives, and (5) eval-
    uating the system after it has been in place for a year or two in
    order to make recommendations on how to improve it.*

11. **What is the hardest part of implementing MBO?**

    *Writing objectives. This is difficult and frustrating, particularly
    when getting started. Quantifying outcomes and writing objec-
    tives is the heart of the system.*

12. **Can MBO be used with clerical, custodial, and student employees?**

    *Yes, it can. Some colleges are using it at this level and with suc-
    cess. The process may need to be modified somewhat to effec-
    tively use it at these levels. For example, more direction should
    come from above in setting objectives; however, the MBO pro-
    cess applied at these levels can have the same advantages that ap-
    ply to the faculty and administrative positions.*

Chapter 15

SUMMARY

This MBO book has been written in an attempt to show the reader what MBO is, where it has come from, why it is needed, how it is applied, and how it can be of significant help in managing the educational enterprise.

The publication is based on the practical experience McManis Associates, Inc. and Dr. Harvey have had in a series of national MBO workshops and in implementing the concept in a number of colleges and universities. It has been written in a brief, concise form so that the busy administrator, trustee, professor, or graduate student may be introduced to the MBO concept without a major investment of time.

Those desiring to know more about MBO are invited to continue their study of the concept by selecting readings from the numerous books and articles listed in the bibliography which follows. Although many of these articles are written from the standpoint of business and industry, the enlightened reader can make appropriate applications to the educational situation.

APPENDIX A

OUTCOME MEASURES DEVELOPED BY A
MIDWESTERN COMMUNITY COLLEGE

**OUTCOME MEASURES DEVELOPED BY A
MIDWESTERN COMMUNITY COLLEGE**

1.00.00.00	**STUDENT GROWTH AND DEVELOPMENT**
1.10.00.00	**General Education and Knowledge**
.01.00	Students Completing Requirements for General Pre-Baccalaureate Programs
.01	Associate in Arts and Associate in Science degrees awarded each year by career center. (AA, AS, and AAS degrees awarded to foreign and out-of-district graduate students.)
.02.00	Transfer of Credits to Other Institutions
.01	Transcripts of credits forwarded to other institutions each year.
.02	Students transferring from college who have been offered scholarships, grants and awards each year.
.03.00	Participation in Non-credit Campus Educational Experiences
.01	Students attending college-sponsored cultural and recreational activities each term.
.02	Students attending college-sponsored non-credit workshops and seminars each term.
.03	Students completing courses for non-credit (audit) by development center each term.
.04.00	Programs for Non-Traditional Students.
.01	Credits earned each term by students classified as "C" on admissions form.
.02	Credits earned each term in courses offered before 8:00 a.m., between 4:00 and 7:00 p.m. and on weekends (Sat. and Sun.).
.03	Persons over 60 years of age completing courses each term.
.05.00	Impact of College Educational Experience on Student's Perception of Man and Society
.01	Selected students' social, political and racial attitudes measured during first term of attendance at college and at time of graduation.
.06.00	Measures of Students' Ability to Communicate Effectively
.01	Graduating students' scores on test indicating their ability to read.

.02   Graduating students' scores on tests that indicate their ability to write.

.03   Graduating students' scores on tests that indicate their ability to communicate orally.

1.20.00.00   **Specialized Skills and Knowledge**

.01.00   Students Completing Requirements in Technical Education

.01   Students successfully completing certificate programs each year by field of specialization.

.02   Students graduating from AAS degree programs each year by field of specialization.

.03   Students passing certification or licensing exams each year.

.02.00   Employment of Graduates of Certificate and AAS Degree Programs

.01   Graduates who are employed in their area of preparation within three months after completion of training.

.02   Graduates who take a first job outside of their area of specialization each year.

.03   Starting salaries of graduates of certificate and AAS degree programs each year.

1.30.00.00   **Satisfaction with College Support Activities**

.01.00   Student Recommendations

.01   Students who recommend attendance at college to friends and relatives measured every two years.

.02   Students attending college on the recommendation of a student or former student measured every two years.

.02.00   College Placement Service

.01   Placement of students in off-campus jobs before graduation.

.02   Students registered with placement service each year.

.03   Job interviews scheduled for marketing graduates each year.

.03.00   Impact of Student Aids

.01   Graduates who received scholarships, grants or aid during last year of attendance at college by amount of aid and source.

.02   Graduates who received scholarships, grants or aid during first year of attendance at college by amount of aid and source.

.03   Funds given to students in direct grants or scholarships each year.

.04   Monies paid to students for part-time on-campus employment each year.

2.00.00.00   **FACULTY AND STAFF DEVELOPMENT**

2.10.00.00   **Work Satisfaction**

.01.00   Working Conditions

.01   Communications initiated each year stating unfair treatment or adverse working conditions as cause.

.02   Resignations each year stating dissatisfaction with working conditions by job classification.

.03   In-house transfers each year by organizational unit.

.04   Changes in pay status made each year (other than normal contractual).

.05   Mandays lost each year to strikes and work stoppages.

.06   Mandays lost each year due to unauthorized absence from duty.

.02.00   Career Growth Opportunities

.01   Employees on leave to other institutions each year by job classification.

.02   Employees granted in-house promotions each year.

.03   Employees on sabbatical leaves each year.

.04   Employees enrolled for credit in other academic institutions each year by job classification.

.05   Financial grant and/or stipends received by employees each year by source of funds.

.06   Participants in college in-service training programs each year by job classification.

.07   Persons participating in tuition waiver program.

3.00.00.00   **COMMUNITY DEVELOPMENT AND SERVICE**

3.10.00.00   **Community Education Development**

.01.00   Affect of Job-Related Educational Experiences of Non-Classified College Students

.01   Non-classified students who receive promotions as result of job-related educational experience each year.

.02   Non-classified students who receive salary increases as a result of job-related educational experience each year.

.03   Non-classified students who obtained new jobs as a result of job-related educational experience each year.

3.20.00.00   **Community Services**

.01.00   Institutional Resources Allocated to Community Service

.01   Budget allocated to community services each year.

.02   Estimated monetary value of community services rendered each year by type of service.

.02.00   Individuals Served by College

.01   Persons attending extra-mural, cultural and recreational activities each year who are not students or employees of the college.

.02   Community residents not associated with college as students or employees who received services from the college each year by type of service rendered.

3.30.00.00   **Community Impact**

.01.00   Employment and Distribution of Students

.01   Graduates employed in college service area measured every three years.

.02   Distribution of college graduates by geographical areas measured every three years.

.03   Annual salary granted college graduates by selected employers measured every three years.

.02.00   Economic Impact

.01   Dollar amount of goods and services purchased by college from service area every year by type of purchase.

.02   Impact of college on decisions to locate business within the service area measured every fifth year.

.03   Estimated annual expenditures determined every three years.

.04   Contracted services with community agencies each year.

4.00.00.00   **PRODUCTS DEVELOPMENT AND UTILIZATION**

4.10.00.00   **Educational Materials, Products, and Reports**

.01.00   Publications by Faculty and Students

.01   Publications by college faculty by type of publication reported each year.

.02   Publications by students by type of publication reported each year.

.03   Publications of college staff used in college classes each year.

.02.00   Educational Products

.01   Educational products (other than publications) developed by college personnel in use on campus each year by type of product.

.02   Technical inventions, patents, technical improvements on existing machines and devices by college faculty, staff, and students reported each year.

.03.00   Development and Research.

.01   Funds allocated to development and research each year.

.02   Developmental and/or research projects completed each year.

4.20.00.00   **Management Information and Reports**

.01.00   Institutional Planning

.01   Research projects completed each year.

.02   Institutional objectives met each year.

.03   Program level objectives met each year.

.04   Dropouts before any credits are earned each term.

.05   Students who do not reenter the institution after absence of one term.

4.30.00.00   **Public Information Materials and Reports**

.01.00   Employer Awareness of College Job Applicants

.01   Employers contacted for job openings each term.

.02   Employers requesting job applicants from college graduates.

.02.00   General Public Awareness of College Institutional Program and Services

.01   News releases which are used by newspapers, radio and/or TV each month.

.02   News releases devoted to student accomplishments which are used by newspapers, radio, and/or TV each term.

.03   News releases devoted to faculty and administrator accomplishments which are used by newspapers, radio and/or TV each term.

.04   Individuals and groups visiting college campus each month.

.05   College publications (including brochures, catalogs, etc.) printed and distributed each year.

.06   Individuals enrolled who learned something about the college or its programs via mass media every three years.

.03.00   Articulation with Community Institutions

.01   Visits to area high schools by college personnel each year.

.02   College programs and presentations to community groups and institutions each year.

.03   Articulation meetings between college staff and baccalaureate granting institutions each year.

APPENDIX B

COMMUNITY COLLEGE MISSION AND GOALS STATEMENTS

COMMUNITY COLLEGE MISSION AND GOALS STATEMENTS

(AUTHOR'S NOTE: Appendix B is a modified mission and goals statement applicable to a community college and listing goals in the three categories mentioned earlier in the guide: educational program, educational impact and operational.)

The mission of Everyone's Community College is to serve as the public comprehensive community college for the residents of its legally defined district. The college will offer programs with a duration of two years or less and will include post-high school vocational, technical and career programs, transfer programs, adult and continuing education programs, community services, and developmental education. The college will also offer a full range of services to assist the students in their development and to complement and supplement the academic program. The college will have an open door admissions policy, will offer programs at the lowest possible cost to students, and is committed to serving a broad range of traditional and non-traditional student needs. Programs will be based on assessed community needs with full accountability to the college constituents. The college is committed to carrying out its educational and administrative tasks with the most modern and effective educational and management techniques in an environment of democratic decision-making. The college will carry out its mission without discrimination against race, color, sex, creed, or national origin in any of its human relationships.

In accomplishing this mission, Everyone's Community College will seek to fulfill the following goals:

EDUCATIONAL — IMPACT

1.   To provide each student with the knowledge and skills necessary to be an independent self-learner.

2.   To provide each student with the necessary skills to become an effective problem solver.

3.   To assist each student in clarifying their values and philosophy of life.

4   To provide students with the knowledge and understanding necessary to live effectively in the future.

5.   To provide students completing certificate programs with the skills and knowledge necessary to be successfully employed in their areas of preparation.

6.   To provide associate degree recipients with the knowledge and skills to be successfully employed in their areas of preparation or to successfully transfer to a senior college.

7.   To enrich the lives of community residents and students by offering cultural programs, short courses, workshops, and other education events of interest to them.

8.   To provide each graduate with the knowledge and skills for healthful living.

9.   To provide each student with the knowledge, skills, and appreciations necessary to effectively use their leisure time.

EDUCATIONAL – PROGRAM

10. To offer a comprehensive curriculum made up of a broad range of certificate and degree programs based on the needs of the citizens of the Everyone's Community College district.

11. To offer a full range of career programs, based on the defined manpower needs of district and state.

12. To provide the first two years of a college transfer program and to maintain a close articulation with four-year institutions to ensure that students will be able to transfer without loss of credit and with a maximum opportunity for success.

13. To provide continuing education and community services for the citizens of the college district by serving as an educational and cultural center.

14. To seek to individualize and humanize the programs of the college in order to meet individual needs and provide students with the maximum opportunity to grow personally, socially, academically, and professionally.

15. To maintain an open-door admissions policy and to offer programs at the lowest possible cost, to make the college accessible to all.

16. To provide counseling, developmental and compensatory education, placement, program planning, and other supportive student services to facilitate student growth and to ensure student success in the academic, social and economic community.

17. To encourage experimentation with new educational methods and to seek to increase the quality and productivity of educational services through the use of sound educational delivery systems.

OPERATIONAL

18. To regularly study the needs of the community and students and to base college goals, objectives, and programs on these needs.

19. To clearly state and periodically review the mission and goals of the college.

20. To annually set quantifiable institutional objectives and report progress to the community.

21. To administer the college with the latest management techniques as efficiently and effectively as possible.

22. To maintain full fiscal accountability and to annually keep expenditures within available revenues.

23. To maintain an effective plan for decision-making and participatory campus governance within the framework of collective bargaining.

24. To maintain effective communication and cooperation between all segments of the campus community and to work together in an environment of mutual trust and respect.

25. To maintain an ongoing program of evaluation for programs and all individuals within the college, focusing on clearly stated quantifiable objectives linked to the mission and goals of the college.

26. To make the facilities and resources of Everyone's Community College available to the citizens of the college district for their educational and recreational use.

27. To provide personal and professional growth opportunities for faculty, administrators, staff and other members of the college community.

28. To carry out an affirmative action employment program and to guarantee equal employment opportunity to all.

APPENDIX C

SAMPLES OF COLLEGE AND UNIVERSITY
ONE- AND FIVE-YEAR OBJECTIVES

SAMPLES OF COLLEGE AND UNIVERSITY
ONE- AND FIVE-YEAR OBJECTIVES

Following are samples of one- and five-year objectives for a college or university. Developmental and maintenance objectives are intermingled but identified with a (D) or an (M) following each objective. All objectives will be accomplished by July 1st of the appropriate year unless otherwise stated.

ONE-YEAR OBJECTIVES

A. Educational Impact

1. Each student graduating with a B.A. degree will be able to pass a nationally standardized reading test at a minimum level of Grade 13. (M)

2. Each student graduating with a B.A. degree will be able to pass a standardized consumer's mathematics test developed by the math department at the 80th percentile or better. (M)

3. Each graduate of the B.A. program will be able to pass a written test on human relations developed by the college at the 75th percentile or better. (M)

4. Each A.A. degree recipient will be able to pass a nationally standardized test on healthful living at the 60th percentile or better. (M)

5. Each student at the college will participate in one intra-mural athletic program each semester. (M)

B. Educational Program

6. The college will offer the B.A. degree with majors in the following areas: _____ , _____, _____, etc. (M)

7. The college will offer A.A. degree programs with concentrations in the following areas: _____, _____, etc. (M)

8. The college will offer community service programs based on assessed community needs and have 2,000 class registrations, (D) if an increase over the previous year.

C. Operational Objectives

9. Carry out a full review of the basic aims and objectives of the college and revise as needed by April 1st. (D)

10. Receive the final report of the Task Force on College Governance and implement a new or revised form of college governance by July 1st. (D)

11. Complete a full review of college personnel policies regarding faculty, administration, and classified staff and make any necessary policy recommendations to the board by May 1st. (D)

12. Develop a revised affirmative action program for the college and submit it to the Federal Government by January 1st. (D)

13. Review all computer reports by functional area used for administrative purposes and recommend revisions by February 1st. (M)

14. Continue the development of management by objectives and prepare the staff for full implementation by July 1st. (D)

15. Develop a foreign travel program for the college and recommend to the board for approval by December 1st. (D)

16. Develop five-year programs and staffing options for all major areas of the college by April 1st. (D)

17. Develop, present, and implement a new faculty evaluation and promotion system by May 1st. (D)

18. Develop a proposal for a comprehensive developmental studies program involving all academic areas and all appropriate areas of student personnel services. (D)

19. Prepare a thorough study of the instructional programs and options of the college and recommend a new model for presentation in the college catalog. (D)

20. Review the college general education requirements in light of the recent state board modifications in the General Education Program and make any desirable recommendations regarding changes in the college program. (D)

FIVE-YEAR OBJECTIVES

1. Fully implement the MBO and PPBS systems by the _____
    college year. (D)

2. Increase the number of vocational-technical programs and options
    by at least 50% over the current year's level. (D)

3. Implement an affirmative action program which will provide a
    staffing pattern in all areas of the college at least equal to the ra-
    cial balance in the county population. (D)

4. Double the Federal funds coming to the college over the current
    year's level. (D)

5. Select and obtain board approval for the site for a third campus
    in the northern part of the county. (D)

6. Increase the percentage of county residents on the professional
    faculty and staff from 65% to 85%. (D)

7. Study and make a recommendation to the board on the establish-
    ment of a college radio and/or TV station. (D)

8. Implement instruction by objectives (IBO) and have at least 30%
    of the college courses taught in this manner. (D)

9. Study the addition to the college of any cooperative programs
    that are feasible and add at least three new programs. (D)

10. Increase the number of students included in the educational pro-
    grams at the college to twenty-two (22) students per 1,000 popu-
    lation in college service areas. (D)

APPENDIX D

MBO READINESS INVENTORY

MBO READINESS INVENTORY

(AUTHOR'S NOTE: Appendix D contains an MBO Readiness Inventory developed by the author for use as a device for taking a quick "snapshot" of staff attitudes regarding MBO. The instrument has some limitations; however, it is a good instrument for looking at a total group and for gaining information for individual interview sessions. The instrument has a self-scoring answer sheet which is also enclosed.)

The following pages contain a brief Management by Objectives (MBO) Readiness Inventory. It takes an average of ten to fifteen minutes to complete. Please complete the inventory, answering each question as you currently feel about the issue. Since this is an attitude inventory, there are no "right" or "wrong" answers. However, the instrument will be scored in accordance with the consultants' perceptions of attitudes harmonious with and consistent with the successful implementation of MBO.

L. James Harvey
Director, Education Division
McManis Associates, Inc.
Washington, D.C.

PLEASE COMPLETE THE FOLLOWING INFORMATION

1. Name _____

2. Check area of college: _____ President's Office   _____ Academic
                                         and Staff   Affairs

                                    _____ Student Affairs   _____ Community
                                                                    Affairs

                                    _____ Other   _____ Business Affairs

3. Have you ever attended a workshop on MBO that lasted a half-day or longer?   _____ Yes   _____ No

4. How would you rate your current level of knowledge of MBO? Please check one.

   _____ Very knowledgeable   _____ Some knowledge

   _____ Knowledgeable   _____ Slight knowledge

   _____ No knowledge

MBO READINESS INVENTORY

by L. James Harvey

The following questionnaire is designed to assess the attitudes of Professional Staff on certain management principles related to the successful implementation of Management by Objectives.

In scoring this questionnaire, points are deducted for divergent responses, and higher point values are awarded to extreme responses (SA and SD).

Please indicate your responses on the following basis:

SA	**A**	**NS**	**D**	**SD**
Strongly Agree	Agree	Not Sure	Disagree	Strongly Disagree

_____ 1. It is just as important today for a large organization to have an effective management system as it is to have good people.

_____ 2. Public service organizations need to focus more on their outcomes than on their activities.

_____ 3. Developing comprehensive twenty-year plans is an outdated activity.

_____ 4. A good executive will, whenever possible, delegate both authority and responsibility for work to subordinates.

_____ 5. A good administrator will give subordinates more objectives and work than they can possibly achieve.

_____ 6. The administrators and professional staff in any public service organization have a right to the final determination of the mission and goals of the organization.

_____ 7. The clearer the idea one has of what one is trying to accomplish, the greater the chances of achieving it.

_____ 8. In public service organizations, it is not practical to give special rewards and/or recognition to those who achieve or produce above the average.

_____ 9. Work will be done most effectively and efficiently if an administrator lays it out in great detail for his subordinates.

_____ 10.   An organization should not spend time and money giving employees information about the organization that is unrelated to
their specific work.

_____ 11.   Planning should be a function of every administrator and it
should be built into the operational level of an organization.

_____ 12.   Employees are more effective and satisfied if they understand
the goals of the organization and how their work fits into the
total picture.

_____ 13.   Public service organizations are so much different from business
and industry that management tools and techniques from business and industry are inappropriate to public service organizations.

_____ 14.   People are so complex that any public service organization which
focuses on helping people cannot expect to be able to quantify
the outcomes of its efforts.

_____ 15.   The professional growth of administrators should have a high
priority in any organization.

_____ 16.   The less clear one's objectives, the more difficult it is to be accountable for what one is doing.

_____ 17.   Mutual trust and confidence between administrators is strengthened when job responsibilities are clearly defined and accountability is firmly established.

_____ 18.   Change and complexity in society are occurring at such a rate
that public service organizations require new management strategies to keep up.

_____ 19.   Anyone who is intelligent enough to have a graduate degree
has the knowledge and skills necessary to be an effective administrator.

_____ 20.   An organization should give a higher priority to the needs of its
employees than it does to accomplishing its goals and objectives.

_____ 21.   The best decisions in a large organization are usually those made
closest to where the "action is."

_____ 22.   In the future, the most successful organizations will be those
which can effectively adapt to change.

_____ 23. Most public service administrators currently work at or near their top level of productivity.

_____ 24. Participative management cannot work effectively in large public service organizations.

_____ 25. Each administrator should have the final authority regarding his objectives and methods.

SCORING OF MBO READINESS INVENTORY

Please check one: _____ Faculty   _____ Administrator

                     _____ Trustee   _____ Other

COLUMN NO. 1			COLUMN NO. 2		
QUESTION NUMBER	YOUR ANSWER	YOUR SCORE	QUESTION NUMBER	YOUR ANSWER	YOUR SCORE
1.	_____	_____	5.	_____	_____
2.	_____	_____	6.	_____	_____
3.	_____	_____	8.	_____	_____
4.	_____	_____	9.	_____	_____
7.	_____	_____	10.	_____	_____
11.	_____	_____	13.	_____	_____
12.	_____	_____	14.	_____	_____
15.	_____	_____	19.	_____	_____
16.	_____	_____	20.	_____	_____
17.	_____	_____	23.	_____	_____
18.	_____	_____	24.	_____	_____
21.	_____	_____	25.	_____	_____
22.	_____	_____			

In Column No. 1 score as follows: SA = +2 A = +1 NS = 0 D = -1 SD = -2

In Column No. 2 score as follows: SD = +2 D = +1 NS = 0 A = -1 SA = -2

Total of + answers   = _____

Less - answers   = _____

TOTAL SCORE   = _____

SCORE INTERPRETATION

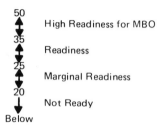

50 High Readiness for MBO

35 Readiness

25 Marginal Readiness

20 Not Ready

Below

MANAGEMENT BY OBJECTIVES BIBLIOGRAPHY

A bibliography of books and articles on MBO and related topics in the education and business fields.

*Most highly recommended sources.

BOOKS

Balderson, Frederick E. **Managing Today's University.** San Francisco: Jossey-Bass, Inc., 1974.

Banghart, Frank W. **Educational Systems Analysis.** New York: Mac-Millan, 1969.

Bass, Bernard M., and Samuel D. Deep. **Current Perspectives for Managing Organizations.** Englewood Cliffs, New Jersey: Prentice-Hall, 1970.

Beck, Arthur C., and Ellis D. Hillman, Eds. **A Practical Approach to Organization Development Through MBO.** Reading, Massachusetts: Addison-Wesley, 1972.

*Beckhard, R. **Organization Development: Strategies and Models.** Reading, Massachusetts: Addison-Wesley, 1969.

Bennis, Warren G. **Organization Development: Its Nature, Origins, and Prospects.** Reading, Massachusetts: Addison-Wesley, 1969.

Bloom, Benjamin S., Ed. **Taxonomy of Educational Objectives.** New York: David McKay Company, Inc., 1965.

*Carnegie Commission on Higher Education. **Papers on Efficiency in the Management of Higher Education.** New York: McGraw-Hill, September, 1972.

Churchman, Charles West. **The Design of Inquiring Systems: Basic Concepts of Systems and Organizations.** New York: Basic Books, 1971.

Churchman, Charles West. **The Systems Approach.** New York: Delacorte Press, 1968.

*Deegan, Arthur X., and Roger Fritz. **MBO Goes to College.** Boulder, Colorado: Division of Continuing Education, Bureau of Independent Study, 1975.

Deegan, William L., and Others. **Community College Management by Objectives.** Sacremento, California: California Junior College Association, 1974.

Desatnick, Robert L. **A Concise Guide to Management Development.** American Management, Inc., 1970.

*Drucker, Peter F. **Management: Tasks, Responsibilities, Practices.** New York: Harper and Row, 1974.

Hartley, Harry J. **Educational Planning - Programming - Budgeting.** Englewood Cliffs, New Jersey: Prentice-Hall, 1968.

Harvey, L. James. **Management by Objectives in Higher Education – A Guide to Implementation.** Washington, D.C.: McManis Associates, Inc., 1974.

Hartnett, R.T. **Accountability in Higher Education: Some Problems in the Assessment of College Impacts.** Princeton: College Entrance Examination Board, 1971.

Hostrop, Richard W. **Managing Education for Results.** Homewood, Illinois: ETC Publications, 1973.

Humble, John W. **Management by Objectives in Action.** London: McGraw-Hill, 1970.

Huff, Robert A. **Inventory of Educational Outcomes and Activities.** Boulder, Colorado: Western Interstate Commission for Higher Education, 1971.

Kast, Fremont Ellsworth. **Organization and Management: A Systems Approach.** New York: McGraw-Hill, 1969.

Kelly, William F. **Management Through Systems and Procedures: The Total Systems Concept.** New York: Wiley-Interscience, 1969.

Kobayashi, Shigeru. **Creative Management.** New York: American Management Association, 1971.

*Lahti, Robert. **Innovative College Management.** San Francisco: Jossey-Bass, Inc., 1973.

Likert, Rensis. **New Patterns of Management.** New York: McGraw-Hill, 1961.

Mager, Robert F. **Preparing Instructional Objectives.** Palo Alto, California: Pacific Book Publishers, 1968.

Mali, Paul. **Managing by Objectives.** New York: Wiley-Interscience, 1972.

Mansergh, Gerald G., Ed. **Dynamics of Management by Objectives for School Administrators.** Danville, Illinois: Interstate Printers and Publishers, 1971.

Marvin, Philip. **Management Goals: Guidelines and Accountability.** Illinois: Dow Jones-Irwin, Inc., 1968.

Marvin, Philip. **Multiplying Management Effectiveness.** New York: American Management Association, 1971.

Metropolitan Detroit Bureau of School Studies, Inc. **Dynamics of Management by Objectives for School Administrators.** Danville, Illinois: Interstate Printers and Publishers, 1971.

*Micek, Sidney S., Allan Service, and Yong S. Lee. **Outcome Measures and Procedures Manual, Field Review Edition.** Technical Report No. 70, Boulder, Colorado: NCHEMS, 1975.

Morrisey, George L. **Management by Objectives and Results.** Massachusetts: Addison-Wesley Publishing Co., 1970.

*Odiorne, George S. **Management by Objectives.** New York: Pitman Publishing Corporation, June, 1972.

*Odiorne, George S. **Management by Objectives: A System of Managerial Leadership.** New York: Pitman Publishing Corporation, 1965.

Odiorne, George S. **Management Decisions by Objectives.** Englewood Cliffs, New Jersey: Prentice-Hall, 1969.

Odiorne, George S. **Personnel Administration by Objectives.** Homewood, Illinois: R.D. Irwin, 1971.

Odiorne, George S. **Training by Objectives:** ⸗ **Economic Approach to Management Training.** New York: MacMillan, 1970.

Olsson, David E. **Management by Objectives.** Palo Alto, California: Pacific Book Publishers, 1968.

*Raia, Anthony. **Managing by Objectives.** Glenview, Illinois: Scott Foresman Co., 1975.

Reddin, William J. **Effective Management by Objectives: The 3-D Method of MBO.** New York: McGraw-Hill, 1971.

Schleh, Edward C. **Management by Results.** New York: McGraw-Hill, 1971.

Stokes, Paul M. **A Total Systems Approach to Management Control.** New York: American Management Association, 1968.

Tanner, C. Kenneth. **Designs for Education Planning.** Lexington, Massachusetts: D.C. Heath and Co., 1971.

Valentine, Raymond F. **Performance Objectives by Managers.** 1966.

*Varney, Glenn H. **Management by Objectives.** Illinois: The Dartnell Corporation, 1971.

Whisler, Thomas L., and Sharley F. Harper, Eds. **Performance Appraisal.** New York: Holt, Rinehart, and Winston, 1962.

Young, Stanley. **Management: A System Analysis.** Illinois: Scott Foresman Co., 1966.

PERIODICALS

Baxter, J.D. "Managing by Objectives' Surfaces," **Iron Age, 100,** (September 25, 1969), pp.98-100.

Bieser, J.E. "Management by Objectives or Appraisals and Results," **Data Management, VIII,** (April, 1970), pp. 24-25.

Birch, A. "Institutional Research is Feedback Between Administration and Management," **College and University Business, IL,** (November, 1970), pp. 28-30.

Byars, Lloyd L. "System Management — What Is It?" **Training and Development Journal, XXVI,** (January, 1972), pp. 32-34.

Carroll, Stephen T., Jr., and Henry L. Tosi. "Goal Characteristics and Personality Factors in a Management by Objectives Program," **Administrative Science Quarterly, XV, 3,** (September, 1970), pp. 295-305.

Carroll, Stephen T., Jr., and Henry L. Tosi. "The Relationship of Characteristics of the Review Process to the Success of the Management by Objectives' Approach," **Journal of Business, XLIV, 3,** (1971), pp. 299-305.

Carroll, Stephen T., Jr., and Henry L. Tosi. "Some Structural Factors Related to Goal Influence in the Management by Objectives Process,"
MSU Business Topics, (Spring, 1969), pp. 45-50.

Curtis, William H. "Program Budgeting Design for Schools Unveiled with
Much Work Still to Go," Nation's Schools, LXXXIV, (November,
1969), pp. 40-43.

Cyphert, Frederick R., and Walter L. Gant. "The Delphi Technique: A
Tool for Collecting Opinions in Teacher Education," Journal of
Teacher Education, XXI, (Fall, 1970), pp. 417-425.

Frank, Edmund R. "Motivation by Objectives — A Case Study," Research
Management, XII, 6, (November, 1969), pp. 391-400.

*Fuller, Jack W. "Continuing Education by Objectives," Journal of Continu-
ing Education, VI, 3, (December, 1971), pp. 175-180.

Gill, J., and C.F. Molander. "Beyond Management by Objectives," Personnel Management, II, (August, 1970), pp. 18-20.

Graves, Clare W. "Levels of Existence: An Open System Theory of Values,"
Journal of Humanistic Psychology, X, 2, (Fall, 1970), pp. 131-155.

*Groth, David. "Administration's Achilles Heel," Community and Junior
College Journal, Volume 44, (October, 1973), pp. 28-30.

Hacker, Thorne. "Management by Objectives for Schools," Administrator's
Notebook, XX, 3, (November, 1971), pp. 1-4.

*Harvey, L. James. "Administration by Objectives in Student Personnel Pro-
grams," Journal of College Student Personnel, (July, 1972), pp. 293-
296.

Henry, Harold W. "Management by Objectives," Tennessee Survey of Business, VI, 3, (November, 1970), p. 13.

Howell, R.A. "Managing by Objectives — A Three Stage System," Business
Horizons, XIII, (February, 1970), pp. 41-45.

Humble, John W. "Management by Objectives," Director, XXII, (November,
1969), pp. 275-280.

Ingraham, W.W., and J.E. Keefe. "Values on Management by Objectives,"
School Management, 16, (June, 1972), pp. 28-29.

Ivancevich, John M. "A Longitudinal Assessment of Management by Objectives," **Administrative Science Quarterly, XVII, 1,** (March, 1972), pp. 126-138.

Ivancevich, John M., James H. Donnelly, and Herbert L. Lyon. "A Study of the Impact of Management by Objectives on Perceived Need Satisfaction," **Personnel Psychology, XXIII, 2,** (1970), pp. 139-152.

*Lahti, Robert E. "Implementing the System Means Learning to Manage Your Objectives," **College and University Business, LII, 2,** (February, 1972), pp. 43-46.

*Lahti, Robert E. "Management by Objectives," **College and University Business, LI,** (July, 1971), pp. 31-32.

Lasagna, John R. "Make Your MBO Pragmatic," **Harvard Business Review, IL,** (November — December, 1971), pp. 64-69.

Levinson, Harry. "Management by Objectives: A Critique," **Training and Development Journal, XXVI, 4,** (April, 1972), p. 38.

Levinson, Harry. "Management by Whose Objectives?" **Harvard Business Review, XLVIII,** (July — August, 1970), pp. 125-134.

Mahler, Walter R. "Management by Objectives: A Consultant's Viewpoint," **Training and Development Journal, XXVI, 4,** (April, 1972), pp. 16-19.

*McConkey, Dale D. "MBO — Twenty Years Later, Where Do We Stand?" **Business Horizons, XIV,** (August, 1973).

*McConkey, Dale D. "The Position and Function of Budgets in an MBO System," **The Business Quarterly,** (Spring, 1974), pp. 44-50.

Minear, Leon P. "Management by Objectives," **American Voactional Journal, XLV,** (December, 1970), pp. 54-55.

Nouri, Clement, Jr., and James I. Fridl. "The Relevance of Motivational Concepts to Individual and Corporate Objectives," **Personnel Journal, XLIX,** (1970), pp. 900-906.

Riggs, Robert O. "Management by Objectives: Its Utilization in the Management of Administrative Performance," **Contemporary Education, XLIII,** (January, 1972), pp. 129-133.

Schrader, Albert W. "Let's Abolish Annual Performance Review," **Management of Personnel Quarterly, VIII, 3,** (1969), pp. 20-30.

Sloan, Stanley, and David E. Schrieber. "What We Need to Know About Management by Objectives," **Personnel Journal, IL,** (March, 1970), pp. 206-208.

Strauss, George. "Management by Objectives: A Critical View," **Training and Development Journal, XXVI, 4,** (April, 1972), pp. 10-15.

Thompson, Paul H., and Gene W. Dalton. "Performance Appraisal: Managers Beware," **Harvard Business Review, XLVIII,** (January — February, 1970), pp. 149-157.

Tosi, Henry L., and others. "Setting Goals in Management by Objectives," **California Management Review, XII,** (Summer, 1970), pp. 70-78.

Wilson, R.A. "Make Objectives Really Come Alive," **Iron Ave, 206,** (August 6, 1970), pp. 52-53.

Wilstrom, Walter S. "Management by Objectives or Appraisal by Results," **The Conference Board Record,** (July, 1966), pp. 27-31.

Wohlking, Wallace. "Management by Objectives: A Critical View," **Training and Development Journal, XXVI, 4,** (April, 1972), p.2.